RICHARD ZEITZ

Plan Smart, Retire Right

A Common Sense Approach to a Stress-Free Retirement

By Richard Zeitz

TABLE OF CONTENTS

ACKNOWLEDGEMENTS

Writing this book has been one of the most fulfilling and rewarding (and not so "stress-free") experiences of my life. Simultaneously, it's been incredibly challenging to write and publish a book while running my practice, and being a husband and father, all at the same time.

As I approached the final stages of *Plan Smart, Retire Right*, I spent some time reflecting on the journey and decisions I've made to reach this pinnacle in my career, as well as the amount of work it took to get this book in front of you. I am deeply grateful to the people that made this book possible, and for those who have encouraged and supported me throughout my life and career. This book is a product of the efforts of hundreds of people, and I feel blessed to be surrounded by such great clients, family and friends.

First and foremost, to my wife, Ally: Most of my "book time" occurred during nights, weekends, while on vacation, and other times inconvenient to our family. Your patience and encouragement during this process has been nothing short of miraculous. Without your consistent support (and first rounds of edits), I'm pretty sure this book would not have been possible. I can never thank you enough for joining me on this journey of life. I love and appreciate you more than you'll ever know.

To my princess, Emily: Loving, caring, and always happy. You are the best daughter a father could ask for. Thank you for putting up with me while I was writing this book. I know we've given up a lot of "daddy-daughter time" this past year and a half, but you have always understood our goal, and have been amazingly tolerant. You've finally got your Papa back! I love you very much.

Enormous gratitude to my loving and caring parents, Howard and Carole, my sister Elysa, and my in-laws, Alex and Alina. A guy couldn't ask for a more supportive family. You've guided and motivated me over the years, giving me the courage to follow my dream of writing this book to share with the world. You've always inspired me to achieve more, and be more, every day. You are my rock(s)!

To my editing, proofreading, publishing, design, and marketing team which comprises a league of superheroes: Kyle Kane, Joshua Iversen, Mike Fallat, Suzana Stankovic, Wesley Tanner and Stacie Sampson. Thank you for your commitment, enthusiasm, and overall awesomeness. *You* deserve the credit for helping me bring this book to market. After countless hours (including Zeitz rantings, blabbering, and "on-the-ride-home chats"), I can truly say this book would've never seen the light of day without your dedication, meticulousness, and expertise. Cheers!

Tom Hegna: A giant in the industry - author, economist, keynote speaker, and a nationally recognized retirement expert. To say that I was honored and ecstatic when you decided to get behind this book is an understatement. Your tremendous work over the years continues to have an impact on many Americans, including myself. Thank you for agreeing to write my foreword. You and your crew are wonderful.

While I'm sure many business owners would say their team is amazing, mine is truly the hallmark of quality. I feel fortunate to have the greatest support team: Catherine Estevez, Michelle Diaz, Adam Sussman, and the stellar back office team at Financial Independence Group. Your "client first" approach has helped us build a strong business, founded on integrity and professionalism. You make me look great every day, and not a moment goes by when I'm not thankful for your commitment to excellence.

When I think about why I choose to do what I do every day, or why I wrote this book in the first place, I can't help but think of all the successes, and the wonderful relationships I've formed along the way. As clients, advocates, and friends, the trust you place in me is a daily reminder of the consistent value I provide. This section is to recognize those whom have added input on the book, and those who have helped make this journey so special:

B&J. Almodovar, R. Amos, E. Attaalla, L. Allen, B. Carter, B. Conlon, B. Deese, D. Duncker, J&A. Esquilin, D&W. Feehrer, L. Finberg, G. Fiorille, R&S. Fishman, J&K. Fitzgerald, A&D. Garcia, K&K. Genalo, O. Ginart, L&E. Gonzalez, M&A. Heinrichs, S&L. Hersh, F&L. Hlavaty, T. Hunt, P&G. Impalla, L&E. Kasauskas, C&C. Keiser, D. Kent, M. Kirschner, M. Kless, E. Kogan, L&A. Kosberg, F. Loganchuk, A. Loprinzi, C&J. Lufrano, V. Majewski, R&I. Marrone, E. McDonnell, C. McFeeley, N&L. McSeed, C&A. Miller, P. Morieko, E&K. Novak, S. Patel, D. Quigley, P. Ramirez, D&D. Sargent, S. Schultz, C. Shinholster, S. Smith, D. Sparano, C. Statum, S. Stranieri, J. Swichar, R&D. Tinari, G&J. Tuballes, S&M. Turtur, J&P. Valenti, M&T. Vatasin, N. Velez, M&M. Waldron, L. Williams

Thank you for giving me the opportunity to express my gratitude!

FOREWORD

I recently visited China, Singapore and Thailand to spend time immersing myself with retirement experts from around the world. Economists, doctors, and executives had all gathered together to learn from each other about retirement and insurance planning. I was invited as a speaker, but I was also able to listen a lot. Upon my return home, I found myself researching some of the material I learned abroad. In the United States, the aging demographic is an interesting phenomenon that I've studied extensively. I was looking for research on other countries that are older. How have other countries dealt with the aging demographic? I came across a shocking story.

An article in *Straits Times* is titled, "Rise in Old Jailbirds Turns Japan Prisons into Retirement Villages." It pointed out that in 2015, a record 47,632 people in Japan aged 65+ were arrested. Over 70% of those arrested were caught for petty crimes such as shoplifting. When retirees have to steal just to survive, it's clear that their plan didn't include enough guaranteed lifetime income to cover their basic living expenses. These people didn't plan at all. What's worse is that Japan's elder inmates are "rehabilitated," kicked back into society, and stuck in the same boat they were before: they haven't gotten any younger, and they still don't have enough income! So, do they get a job and start saving for their slower retirement years?

No, they steal a bunch of bananas for breakfast and get thrown right back into the slammer!

I share this story with you to prove a point. Imagine a retirement plan where prison is the best option for some people. Prison! Now, I'm exaggerating slightly, but how much different is that than potentially running out of money in retirement? Like many Americans, I've worked hard my entire life, from delivering the *Minneapolis Star and Tribune* when I was a boy, to pounding the pavement as an insurance agent during my first few working years in the Arizona desert, all the way to today, where I travel about 200 days a year speaking all over the world. Our hard work deserves more. Unfortunately, hard work without a plan isn't a viable path for retirement. For many Americans, people are simply failing to plan and properly educate themselves regarding how to attain a stress-free retirement.

I had connected with Richard Zeitz a few years back throughout my speaking engagements around the globe. Upon meeting Richard, I could tell immediately, "He GETS it." When he reached out to me later and told me he was writing a book, I was excited to hear his perspective. Little did he know, when he asked me to write this foreword, that I would be writing about people where prison may be their best retirement option!

In the United States, there are more than 78 million baby boomers heading into retirement. There is absolutely no debate that our country is getting older. With the massive government debt lurking on the horizon, we are entering an era where people cannot count entirely on government sponsored programs. You must plan for retirement on your own for the sake of your family and future generations.

In my years of studying retirement, I have found that there are really two key components to a successful retirement: #1. Increasing income to last for the rest of your life, and #2. Risk management – taking all the key retirement risks off the table. If you focus on those two key items, you are much more likely to have a happy and successful retirement. Richard lays this out and clearly demonstrates WHY a proper retirement plan can be the difference between achieving your long-term financial goals, or not.

See, most people think retirement is about the size of their 401k, the stock market, or the value of their real estate assets. While each of those can play a part, NONE of them can ensure a successful retirement. Much more importantly: How much guaranteed lifetime income do you have? How can you get the most out of your Social Security benefit? What is your plan for inflation protection? How can you guard against market risk? What is your plan for long-term care? How can you best leave a legacy to your family or favorite charity? Have you thought about how an increasing tax rate environment might affect your 401k and IRA withdrawals? Your answers to these questions are far more important than the ups and downs of the stock market, or the total value of your assets.

Retirement planning around the world faces unique challenges. Here in this book, Richard has gathered evidence and outlines strategies that can help you radically improve your retirement outcomes. Richard does an incredible job educating his clients on how to best pursue and protect their financial dignity. I hope you will enjoy reading this book as much as I have, and that you take the necessary steps to ensure a successful and stress-free retirement for yourself.

Tom Hegna
Author, Speaker, Economist

INTRODUCTION

Plan Smart, Retire Right.

"An investment in knowledge pays the best interest."
- Benjamin Franklin

Do you realize you could spend as many years in retirement as you did in your working years? According to the Society of Actuaries, as of 2017, the life expectancy for a 65-year-old man is 85.8 years, and 87.8 years for a 65-year-old woman. Further, the individual mortality tables illustrate that one in four 65-year-old men can expect to live until age 93, while one in four 65-year-old women can expect to reach age 96. Let that sink in for a moment. Good news you say, right? Good news indeed. However, generally speaking, people aren't adequately prepared for a long retirement, and without proper planning, they can easily outlive the money they've saved. Do you have a big enough nest egg for retirement? Do you know exactly how much money you'll need to ensure you never outlive your savings?

In the good old days, planning for retirement was pretty simple; people didn't have to worry as much about it because they didn't live far beyond their retirement. You worked for 30 years, received a company pension, and put your money in the bank or invested in savings bonds to make it last. Back in the day, life expectancies were short, and on average, people spent less than a decade in retirement. Planning was relatively easy.

In today's world, retirement planning is considerably different, and more important than ever. The fact is, people are living longer today than at any time in history. And with medical advances in healthcare, science and technology, this "longevity" trend should only gain momentum. A successful retirement plan and sound money management approach can often be the difference between running out of money in retirement, or fulfilling your long-term dreams of financial security.

Are you financially free to do whatever you want, whenever you want, without thinking twice about it? Can you take a spur-of-the-moment vacation, or do you find yourself cutting expenses to the bone because you are worried you won't have enough money to retire? Do you find yourself losing sleep at night because you're worrying about your finances? Do you feel as though you have come to a financial fork-in-the-road that has you asking yourself *what* to do, *how* to do it, *why* to do it, and *when* to do it?

The book you are about to read is filled with strategies and principles intended to not only grow and extend your retirement dollars, but to also protect your money along the way, encouraging you to keep a longevity and risk management approach in mind. Each chapter of this book will provide you with insights, and steps you can take right now to create a stress-free retirement for yourself. This book is intended to help you take control of your financial future and enjoy the retirement you've always dreamed of, while gaining a richer and more fulfilling life.

Don't be the person who goes headlong into retirement without the peace of mind in knowing for certain you've addressed the most common risks to your retirement plan and financial future. Every day you wait to implement the proper plan and the following risk management concepts is another day you could be unknowingly gambling with your financial future. This book will teach you how to take immediate action to plan for, control, and protect your retirement. Be a person who makes it a priority to secure your financial well-being and does so without delay, so you can experience a retirement that allows you to lead the lifestyle you want to lead.

When it comes to retirement planning, it's easy to understand what our financial goals are; however, the more important question to ask yourself is, "Why?". We go through life making decisions every day, but do we ever stop and ask *why* we make these decisions, or how these decisions relate to our larger purpose? What are we trying to achieve, and *why* are we trying to achieve it? Ask yourself *why,* then visualize what a stress-free retirement would look like. What would it mean to attain your financial goals? How would it make you feel? If your goal is to be financially free and live the life you want to live, whether you ever get around to retiring or not, *why* is that the goal? If your goal is to be debt free, you need to understand *why.* While the answers to these questions may seem obvious, it's important to understand the proper order to address them in an effort to maximize your long-term results.

Would you like to examine where you are today financially, and ensure you're doing everything you can to maximize and protect your retirement? If so, this book is for you. *Plan Smart, Retire Right* is about setting you on the right course and helping you map out a strategy to ensure you can live the stress-free retirement you deserve.

This book is for people who are looking to move beyond just having a financial plan in place, and into true financial security. To help you get there, I am providing you with this easy-to-follow guide to build a stress-free retirement. If you follow the strategies in this book, I'm confident you will not only help protect your money from many of life's unforeseen and unexpected events, but you'll also substantially improve your chances of truly experiencing what a stress-free retirement really feels like.

To achieve this, we must first determine what financial security means to you. What does it mean to be financially secure? Different people will answer this question in different ways. Broadly speaking, a serviceable definition of *financial security* means having enough money to live a comfortable lifestyle, no matter how long you live. However, a comfortable lifestyle may mean different things to different people, so let's provide a more precise definition: to be *financially secure* is to have enough money to live a lifestyle *you* find comfortable.

While not the focus of this book, it should be mentioned that other definitions can be used for the concept of financial security. The term is sometimes equated with "financial survival," which is often used to mean simply having enough money for food and shelter. Although this is a minimum requirement for being financially secure, most people aspire to do more than just "survive" in retirement. This book focuses on real strategies designed to help you achieve such an outcome.

As you journey down the road to financial freedom, you'll need to make some difficult choices, and ask yourself an important question: "What path do I need to take to be financially free?" This book is designed to provide you with a blueprint to achieve a truly free financial future.

Financial planning isn't just about where you are now and where you want to be in 5, 10, or 15 years down the road; it's also about the "what if's" in life that happen along the way, each one with the ability to derail the plan you've put into place.

Over the years, many people have come to me with plans that didn't address risk management, plans that weren't able to handle unexpected occurrences which have a tendency to throw things off course. These plans fell short because they only focused on the potential rewards and failed to address the potential risks.

After sharing the information contained in this book with my clients, many have told me that by implementing these same ideas and strategies, their retirement has been enjoyable and stress-free. I believe yours can be too.

What is a Stress-Free Retirement?

A stress-free retirement is one without financial worries in which you can play with your grandkids, travel when you want, fix up your residence, go out to a restaurant without pinching pennies, and live your life the way you want to live. It means you don't have to constantly worry about money, and you can make decisions without having to check your account balance every time you spend a few dollars.

At the end of the day, living the retirement lifestyle you desire means having enough money set aside for a rainy day, and enough positive monthly cash flow to cover your expenses, at a minimum, so you won't run out money during retirement and can deal financially with whatever comes your way. Basically, instead of rolling the dice with your retirement, you set up a well-planned strategy which enables you to adequately *prepare* for retirement. If you are looking for a road map to help improve and simplify your finances to have more confidence throughout your golden years, this book can show you how. In order to achieve a stress-free retirement, you need to change the way you view your savings and investments. This book is about taking a different approach when examining your particular financial situation. Not to say that one point of view is better than another – it's just smart to consider different approaches to financial planning.

Over the years, I've met people who have what many would consider a sizable amount of savings and investments, but wind up having to work later in retirement to keep up with expenses. Merely "having money" does not imply you are *financially secure*. Due to improper planning, excessive risk-taking, and overspending, these people run the risk of being broke in 10 or 20 years. Conversely, I have clients without a large amount of savings and investments, but through a careful and common sense approach to planning, they have portfolios that can last them way beyond age 100.

As a veteran in the financial services industry, I have personally orchestrated hundreds of retirement plans, and have trained many advisors on how to do the same. I am passionate about helping people build a plan that allows them to truly live a stress-free retirement. It's what motivates me to come to work every day. I thrive on the opportunity to show people a smarter way to plan for and optimize their retirement. It's an experience I find extremely rewarding.

It is my mission to help people retire well, to help them build sustainable retirement plans, create more wealth and income, and have more time to do what they want to do. Not a day goes by where I'm not humbled and flattered to work with the people who choose to enlist my services to help them plan for their retirement. They could go anywhere, and they have many options; some even have financial advisors in their families. People choose to work with me and my firm because of the way we simplify their financial affairs, and break down financial planning into easy, doable steps. This book will provide an outline for the steps we take with our clients to build a forward-thinking retirement plan.

A Balanced Approach to Financial Planning

Planning for your retirement can be complicated and overwhelming. Finding the right balance between today's needs and tomorrow's goals is often easier said than done. Financial planning isn't just about putting your money where it will potentially get the best return - it's about understanding the *purpose* of every dollar you have and creating a sound plan to protect your money throughout retirement. This understanding can help you live the life you'd like to experience through a fulfilling retirement.

Here's the thing: planning for retirement doesn't have to be difficult. You don't need to have an Ivy League education, a degree in accounting, or a Masters in Finance to be successful. You also don't need millions in the bank or be the recipient of a trust fund to enjoy your retirement. What you *do* need is common sense, and a desire to take control of your financial future. I want this book to not only provide you with a valuable education, but to inspire you to achieve financial success in retirement.

My goal in this book is to introduce strategies that can help you strike the right balance and manage your investments and savings to help you meet your retirement goals. These strategies, which are based on my knowledge and many years of financial industry experience, can help you define goals and priorities for your money, and take the necessary steps to meet those goals. I'll put the expertise I've developed over the years to work for you through implementing financial strategies designed to simplify your life and instill confidence that your goals for the future will remain within reach.

Think of all the freedom, joy and abundance you could create for yourself in retirement, knowing you've put a smart plan in place for your retirement years. There's no question that the *Plan Smart, Retire Right* approach and strategies described in this book can change your life forever; but, of course, it's up to you to take advantage of them. No matter how much money you have, this book is designed to help you map out a strategy you can understand, follow, and utilize to reach your financial goals. Most importantly, the goal of this book is to show you things you can do right now, to ensure you don't run out of money in retirement.

My clients, whether pre-retirees or already retired, have experienced great success and a more confident and stress-free retirement by implementing the concepts and approaches found in this book. Furthermore, if you find yourself among the ranks of those who aren't sure whether or not you'll be able to retire when you'd like to, this book may answer a lot of the questions you have and help pave the way to a more fulfilling retirement. Who knows, perhaps you'll discover you can actually retire earlier than you might have thought.

Plan Smart, Retire Right is your personal guide to achieving a stress-free and financially fulfilling retirement. Are you ready to get started?

CHAPTER 1

Everyone Needs a Financial Plan

Before we dig in, I'd like to make one thing very clear: financial planning is not just for the wealthy. The thought that you need to be rich in order to benefit from financial planning may be one of the biggest misnomers out there. As a matter of fact, studies show that putting a comprehensive financial plan in place can benefit people at any income level. The good news is there's never a minimum amount you need before you can start, simply because the process of financial planning is not tagged to any specific "magic" number. In my opinion, everyone can benefit from constructing a financial plan, and having a plan should certainly instill more confidence in your retirement.

I think it's important to understand what a financial plan is and why everyone should have one. Let's take look at a general definition of a *financial plan*. According to *Investopedia*, a financial plan is a comprehensive evaluation of an investor's current and future financial state by using currently known variables to predict future cash flows, asset values, and withdrawal plans. Financial planning is about knowing where you currently stand, and then determining what you'd like your future financial state to look like. It's about building an integrated strategy with various types of retirement investments.

As you can imagine, it's not uncommon to feel overwhelmed by the number of important decisions we need to make regarding retirement accounts, investments, college savings and other complicated financial issues that may come our way. For this reason alone, I believe you can benefit from working with a financial advisor to help develop a realistic, measurable, and achievable plan with your specific goals in mind.

Today's financial environment is complex, and in many ways uncertain. The decisions you make regarding career, spending, savings and investments, both now and in the future, can significantly impact your financial situation over the long-term. Hoping or praying that everything will work out the way you expect—whether this involves watching the sunset while sipping daiquiris on a beautiful beach, or simply being able to enjoy all the pursuits you never had time for while working—just isn't enough. Hoping things go well isn't a sound strategy.

Financial planning can help to enhance your knowledge of various topics relative to your current financial situation, and provide a framework for clarifying, structuring and simplifying your financial endeavors. The main goal of financial planning is to help take the uncertainty and guesswork out of managing your finances so you can truly see the big picture and make more informed decisions – thus enabling you to better understand the implications of each financial decision you make. We all have different goals, and no single financial solution is right for everyone. Therefore, it's important to have a customized financial roadmap that works for you and your particular financial situation.

While many people understand that not having a plan in place for retirement is unwise, sometimes this happens because of what is referred to as "paralysis by analysis". Paralysis by analysis occurs when we spend so much time studying every little detail about a decision that we fail to take any action at all. When faced with too much information and too many options, many people take the easy road (whether it's in their best interest or not), which is doing nothing. They become frozen by having too many options. This type of thinking is brought on because we feel as though, by not understanding 100% of what we're doing and why we're doing it, we'll be punished for making mistakes. Fear is the primary culprit of indecisiveness.

Instead of letting an overload of information get in the way and paralyze you into procrastination, learn to focus on what's important. Define your goals, understand your options, eliminate the noise, do more research, then choose the options that best meet your needs. Analysis paralysis is a real and risky phenomenon that can prevent you from achieving your goals, and I have seen it time and time again. But it can be avoided with some thoughtful planning and methodical action. If your advisor has done a thorough job helping you plan, then you should have clear objectives, a list of viable options, and the research to back them up.

The Benefits of Financial Planning

"Planning is bringing the future into the present so you can do something about it now." – Alan Lakein

With the average American facing an uncertain economy, a volatile stock market, and more options for saving and investing than ever before, it's easy to feel confused and overwhelmed. Having a financial plan in place provides structure to your actions, which can help you avoid making costly mistakes. Going into retirement without a plan or strategy can potentially lead to suboptimal results. Without the discipline a plan provides, you may make mistakes that can have damaging long-term effects on your ability to retire, and your retirement lifestyle, even if they don't immediately harm your financial situation.

Financial planning carefully lays out how to best utilize your financial resources, and then put action steps in place to help accomplish your goals. It keeps the purpose of your decisions clear and in focus at all times and helps constantly answer *why* you are doing something. Look at your financial plan as a map or GPS. Imagine you're going on a long journey to a place you've never been, and you don't have a map or GPS to follow. Sure, you can eventually reach your final destination on your own, but it may not be the most efficient path. Many people rely on a map or GPS because we know it usually shows the most direct path to reach our destination, taking into account variables such as traffic, accidents, speed limits, etc. A financial plan is just like using a map or GPS, guiding your finances, retirement and life, while offering a clearer, smoother path to your destination.

Some of the key benefits of financial planning include:

- Getting the correct answers to important questions about your financial goals
- Helping you take the steps necessary to live the lifestyle you want in retirement
- Identifying any potential issues with your current retirement plan, including income gaps
- Demonstrating ways to improve the structure of your retirement income

- Establishing best practices to increase retirement savings
- Providing you with the peace of mind that you are prepared for retirement
- Learning better ways to manage risks in retirement, such as:
  - Outliving your money
  - Rising healthcare costs
  - Inflation
  - Market volatility

If you don't feel confident in your future, and your financial life feels worrisome or seems to be spinning out of control, you're not alone. Today more than ever, financial advisors can be an essential resource. From budgeting, to preparing for retirement, saving for education, and managing your insurance needs, financial planning brings together all the pieces of the challenging puzzle that encompasses planning for the future and managing your finances.

Investing for retirement takes patience and planning. Mastering these traits requires deferring gratification – saving money today so you can spend it when you're retired. Allowing something (anything) to get in the way of successfully exercising patience and productively planning your retirement is a mistake. Here are some of the most common mistakes that can prevent you from achieving your retirement goals.

Procrastination – The Money Killer

It's very easy to find reasons to delay making decisions when it comes to saving and planning, but the one friend you don't have on your side is *time* – once you lose time, it's gone forever. If something unforeseen occurs – for instance, if your retirement plan at work is adjusted to pay out less than you had expected – or your Social Security payments are decreased, you'll have to use your own savings to make up for any shortfall. The more time you give yourself to adjust to the unexpected changes life throws at you, the better equipped you should be to weather such occurrences. And the longer you wait, the less time you have, and the more it can hinder your ability to enjoy a stress-free retirement.

The biggest issue I see with procrastination is that it's a long-term money killer. If you wait too long to invest, you can find yourself faced with having to take a more aggressive approach to investing than you might prefer; one that involves assuming more risk than you're comfortable with, in an attempt to make up for lost time to meet your retirement objectives.

While starting as soon as possible is recommended, it's never too late to save for retirement. Having a plan in place can provide discipline and structure, and can ultimately improve your quality of life down the road. When it comes to setting aside money for your future, it's easy to make excuses to put it off until later. The good news: saving for retirement is a marathon, not a sprint. Don't fall into the procrastination trap. Unless you absolutely must use every penny for current expenses, make it a priority to set aside some portion of each paycheck towards retirement savings.

If you delay in setting aside money for retirement, you make it harder to achieve your goals. Especially during your peak earning years, it's important to save as much as possible for the future. You want to avoid falling short of your retirement target and preferred retirement lifestyle, or being forced to go back to work to make ends meet. There's nothing wrong with working for as long as you like, as long as you enjoy doing so. But, generally speaking, the younger we are, the easier it is to work harder or learn new skills to increase our savings.

This is why it's so important to maximize your savings for retirement while you're in the best position to do so. You can make life easier for yourself in retirement by starting to save as much as possible, as early as possible. Otherwise, you may find yourself not being able to retire or having to work longer than you need.

Aside from this, another good reason to begin saving earlier on in life is the opportunity to take advantage of compound interest over time to maximize the growth of your savings. While saving is a great idea at almost any age, the power of compound interest goes a long way to build up a large nest egg for your future. Obviously, the earlier you start saving, the better off you are in the long run.

The Power of Compound Interest

Compound interest has been called the 8th Wonder of the World – and deservedly so. By earning interest on interest as well as principal, your money grows much faster than it would otherwise. This effect is most noticeable over longer periods of time, when the magic of compounding can cause your total investment return to substantially increase from what it would be using simple interest.

The following examples illustrate this process:

Imagine you have received an inheritance of $50,000. You set this money aside as retirement savings, hoping that it will grow over time and help provide you with income once you retire. If you place these funds in an investment that grows at 8% *simple interest* (how much can you earn on the original amount you invested), the total amount you will have after 5 years is $70,000. If it grows at 8% interest, compounded yearly, the total amount is $73,466.

While the amount you earn with *compound interest* (the amount you earn from your initial investment in addition to the interest you earn, on top of the interest that has already accrued) is greater than with simple interest over this 5-year time period, the true impact of compound interest is best illustrated over longer periods of time. Let's look at the same return scenario (8%), but over 30 years instead of 5; the difference is tremendous! At 8% simple interest, your funds grow to $170,000; while at 8% compound interest, they grow to $503,132!

Simple Interest vs Compound Interest		
	Simple Interest	Compound Interest
Amount Invested	$ 50,000	$ 50,000
Rate of Return	8%	8%
Number of Years	5	5
Investment Earnings	$ 20,000	$ 23,466
Total Value	**$ 70,000**	**$ 73,466**
Amount Invested	$ 50,000	$ 50,000
Rate of Return	8%	8%
Number of Years	30	30
Investment Earnings	$ 120,000	$ 453,132
Total Value	**$ 170,000**	**$ 503,132**

Emotional decisions vs. Practical decisions

"The investor's chief problem, even his worst enemy, is likely to be himself." - Benjamin Graham

---

When markets swing, emotional decision-making can wreak havoc on the most carefully designed investment strategies. Emotions like fear, doubt and greed often control our financial decisions, and play a dominant role in those investment decisions. This is magnified during periods of intense market volatility. Fear can cause us to abandon an investment strategy when the outcome is not what we want. Greed can cause us to chase investment trends and take on too much risk. Unfortunately, when it comes to financial decisions, these emotions can often get in the way of what we must logically do to hit our goal. As a leader of your financial household, just as a leader in any business or organization, you must learn to trust the numbers and make decisions based on facts and logic, rather than emotions.

When examining the results of emotional financial decisions, let's look at the highlights of the financial research provided in 2017 by Dalbar and Associates in its annual study entitled, "Quantitative Analysis of Investor Behavior". The purpose of this study was to examine the common equity behaviors of the average investor. The study illustrated that the general temptation for investors to time the market often resulted in investors diving into the market at the top and fleeing at the bottom. In fact, the study showed that over the 20-year period from 12/31/1996 to 12/31/2016, the S&P 500 Index earned an average of 7.68%, while the individual investor earned an average return of only 4.79%. What does this tell us? It supports the assertion that many investors tend to follow their emotions, and often jump in and out of markets at the wrong times. They do this in an attempt to increase returns or avoid losses, but ultimately cause their investments to substantially underperform market averages through emotionally-driven decisions.

It's been proven that investors often make the wrong moves in the market by investing at the wrong times, often for the wrong reasons. To avoid this type of scenario negatively impacting your financial health and potentially sabotaging your own retirement, you need to have discipline and a better strategy in place. Along with some behavioral coaching, the implementation of tools and strategies outlined in this book can help to ensure you're invested prudently and remain on the right track.

Active, risk-managed strategies are designed to smooth out an investor's ride in the market by addressing volatility and avoiding extreme market movements. This approach helps investors better control their emotions and stick with an investment plan over the long-term, which is especially important for those in or approaching retirement. When working with clients, my role is to reinforce the realities of market cycles and constantly remind them there will often be choppy periods in the markets, both prior to and during retirement. While the plan we've set in place is important, at the end of the day, how an investor handles these various periods are what ultimately matters most.

To make rational decisions, it is important to acknowledge that your emotional responses represent legitimate drives. While giving into uncontrolled greed is not a virtue, the desire to acquire wealth certainly is, from the standpoint of retirement planning. By the same token, while being excessively fearful can be counterproductive when it comes to your finances, if a bit of fear instills caution, that can be a good thing. Investing your hard-earned money recklessly is not a very productive approach to take.

A rational approach to investing is to use the basic human drives underlying these two emotions to form your financial decisions, without letting them hijack the decision-making process. Thus, if you encounter an investment which seems too good to be true—for example, an investment product that promises to offer stratospheric returns with little or no risk—don't give in to greed and part with your hard-earned money without further investigation into the product. Further research, known in the investment world as *due diligence*, can likely yield a result of the old saying, "if it sounds too good to be true, it probably is." In the investment world, above-average returns typically come with above-average risk, no matter what any salesperson tells you.

I'm not saying you should only look for low-risk investments. What I am saying is when investing for retirement with the benefit of a long-term time horizon, it can be advantageous to take some risk in order to receive a higher return. When considering this strategy, it's important to keep your fear in check.

For instance, investing in the stock market via a mutual fund or ETF (an ETF is an exchange-traded fund, which typically seeks to mirror the performance of a market index as closely as possible; for instance, the S&P 500) involves more volatility than simply leaving your money in a savings account or buying a government bond. However, in return for accepting this higher volatility (risk), such investments typically perform better over longer periods of time than savings accounts or other fixed income investments, such as government or corporate bonds. Thus, investing some of your money in growth-oriented mutual funds or ETFs can turn out to be a rational approach when it comes to retirement investing. A financial plan can help bring clarity to your financial situation and assist you in developing a strategy so it's easier to make financial decisions, formulate short-term and long-term goals, and stay on the correct path.

Retirement Analysis

When planning for retirement, due to advancements in medical technology, I believe it makes sense to plan to age 100, at a minimum. When I conduct a retirement analysis for clients, I run many different scenarios to illustrate how our strategies can carry them to at least age 100. If they look as though they are going to fall short with their retirement funds, we make adjustments accordingly. The problem with planning to life expectancy is that it's just an average. What if you actually beat the average? Then what?

Did you know that by using financial planning software, either on your own, or with an advisor's help, you can run projections showing the outcomes of various hypothetical retirement scenarios? When performing initial planning for clients, it's common practice for me to overestimate expenses and underestimate income. This allows me to show them a truer picture of their retirement cash flow in a more conservative light.

By using aggressive expense calculations and conservative income estimates, I am able to show a client how their retirement plan can likely hold up if things don't go as well as they had hoped. While some advisors assume that certain expenses disappear or decrease as you get older, I like keeping expenses at the same level, even increasing in certain areas. In order to reflect the notion that when one expense drops off, it's often replaced by another, we discuss potential expenses that may come up in retirement. For example, while we may pay off some monthly recurring debts as we head into retirement, now that we have retired, we may travel more than usual. Another good example is that as you age, medical costs are likely to increase as you encounter health issues in retirement. Unexpected expenses like these can be devastating.

Some advisors use rosy assumptions to make clients' current retirement plans appear appealing. I believe taking this approach does the client a disservice. In addition to erring on the side of caution when it comes to projecting income and expenses, I also like to present clients with several "what-if" scenarios, including some hypothetical worst-case situations, so that they have a complete picture of the potential outcomes of their retirement plan.

To make this step simpler, I always recommend people perform a retirement portfolio analysis. The software used for this purpose can provide customized reports that look at your income and assets to provide a detailed review of your financial situation. It can highlight your investment strengths and weaknesses, as well as illustrate how long your money could last in retirement. Your financial advisor can then offer recommendations and strategies to help tweak and optimize your financial outlook.

Financial planning software of this type can do things that no human can by rapidly calculating a variety of retirement scenarios, then displaying the results in graphical form within seconds. For instance, you can use the software to test a variety of savings scenarios to determine how much you should set aside each month to hit your desired retirement savings number. It can also show how your retirement income might differ depending on the rate of return on your investments, inflation, and other variables.

These software programs can track both needs-based and goal-based scenarios. They enable you to perform an in-depth examination of your financial situation on a cash flow basis to identify any shortfalls or areas of concern, as well as aiding you in performing the aforementioned future goal projections. If you don't have experience running financial projections or using these types of financial tools, it might make sense to consult a financial advisor for assistance while making forecasts and interpreting potential results related to your particular financial situation. In general, an experienced advisor should be able to help you get the most from your use of financial planning software.

In addition to planning to age 100 and beyond, I also run financial scenarios for my clients that accurately depict the overall risk to their plan in retirement – current risk vs. recommended rebalance. This allows me to calculate an investor's risk tolerance utilizing a scientific framework which fits their unique and individual risk preference to meet their expectations with confidence.

This is extremely helpful when it comes to examining the results of different scenarios and their overall impact on a client's plan. Once we understand which situation is optimal, I believe it's important to "stress test" the plan using different market circumstances and possible simulations to see how the portfolio can hold up against economic events, such as prolonged bear markets, market corrections like those that occurred in 1987, 2001, or 2008, a dramatic spike in interest rates, etc.

When to Use a Financial Advisor

Do you have the time, energy, knowledge, discipline and desire to do financial planning on your own? Some people decide to do their own financial planning and feel as though they understand how to implement the best strategies and products for their retirement. If that's you, great! If not, you may want to seek help from a financial advisor.

A qualified financial advisor can help if you:

- Don't have the time or the resources to do your own financial planning
- Want to better manage your finances but aren't sure where to start
- Need expertise on how to implement good financial planning decisions
- Don't have deep knowledge in areas such as investments, insurance, taxes or retirement planning
- Find the value in having a financial "coach" to help guide you through retirement
- Have an immediate need or unexpected life event

While simply having a plan in place can give you more confidence in retirement, regularly reviewing and updating the plan is extremely important, and greatly enhances the likelihood of achieving your desired results. As an active resource both prior to and in retirement, a competent financial advisor can help you stay on track when it comes to achieving your financial goals, acting as a sounding board when needed, helping to identify and balance your financial goals every year (and making adjustments where necessary), and providing you with timely updates on retirement solutions that can put you in a better overall financial position. Finally, working alongside a financial advisor can help steer you away from potentially harmful, knee-jerk, emotional decisions, keeping you focused on your long-term goals and objectives.

CHAPTER 2

Two Financial Phases

As discussed earlier, every dollar you own has a purpose. To determine the purpose of each dollar, it helps to first identify which financial phase you are currently in. At its most basic element, your financial life can be separated into two distinct phases: accumulation and distribution.

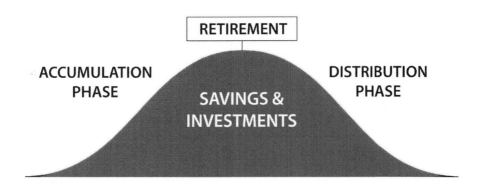

In the accumulation phase, the traditional path is to go to school, get a job and make money, save and grow your money, start a family or some variant thereof; it's all about

42

accumulating assets and accumulating wealth. Whereas in the distribution phase, you've now entered into retirement and put your earning years behind you. Here, you have to wear a different hat and employ a different strategy while going into what I refer to as *asset protection mode.*

Your dollars have a different purpose when you're accumulating them than they do while you're taking distributions from them. During accumulation, the primary purpose is growth; while during distribution, the primary purpose is to provide income. One of the biggest mistakes I frequently see people make is not understanding which of the two money phases they are in. Each of these phases requires a different investment strategy and approach. Not understanding this basic principle and how to manage your money during these distinct phases could be the difference between a fruitful, stress-free retirement, or quite the opposite.

Accumulation Phase vs. Distribution Phase

Mountain climbing is actually a lot like planning for retirement. Let's take a look at the highest mountain in the world, Mount Everest. I once read that 15% of the deaths on Mount Everest occur while climbing to the summit – the ascent – and 85% occur on the climb down – the descent. I often use these statistics with my clients when drawing a parallel between accumulation and distribution.

During the *accumulation (ascent) phase* you are trying to build up as much retirement savings as possible to reach the peak (retirement). During this process, you're working; if any mistakes are made, you've got time on your side, and still have cash flow coming in from your employment. In most cases, you're not really going to miss a beat. Additionally, most of the retirement funds you're building up are not going to be touched until you actually reach your retirement years. However, if missteps are made or if catastrophes out of your control occur during the *distribution (descent) phase*, it can be financially devastating to your overall plan and lifestyle.

While I can't cite the percentage of retirees that fail in the distribution phase, I think this comparison drives home two important points:

1. The typical American, and many financial advisors, focus on the climb up – figuring out the optimal ways to invest and grow money in order to reach the summit (retirement). On the other hand, many people spend little time thinking about the rest of the journey. After years of hard work and saving for retirement, no real plan exists for how to wisely use their nest egg to ensure it lasts throughout retirement – and be sure they make it safely down the mountain.

2. When problems occur on the way down the mountain (distribution), even the greatest financial plan in the world can be at risk of suffering losses that can affect your retirement.

A major objective of this book is to point out methods that can help you descend Mount Everest (a long and financially healthy retirement) safely and stress-free, without jeopardizing all the work you've done (saving for retirement) on the way up. Let's dig into these two phases a bit more.

Accumulation Phase

Grow your money and protect your family

The main purpose of accumulation is to save and grow as much money as possible during your working years, prior to retirement. Typically, a growth strategy works well here and planning is a little easier because your time horizon is known in advance. As you get closer to retirement, you can start thinking about how to protect these funds through different asset allocation strategies and better overall diversification. During the accumulation phase, your goal should be to grow your money to help secure your financial future. This is important not only for achieving family-oriented goals such as purchasing a house or paying for a child's education, but also for accumulating sufficient retirement savings.

Achieving growth during the accumulation phase helps prepare you to successfully enter the next phase of your life: the distribution, or retirement phase. When you retire, your financial flexibility declines, making it much more difficult and risky to invest for growth.

Distribution or Withdrawal Phase

Protect your money, create a lifetime income plan,
leave a legacy

While you'd still want your money to grow during the distribution phase, this is where you ensure you don't run out of money by preparing for "retirement cash flow". At this stage, an adjustment should be made towards a more conservative asset allocation, due to the fact that a big market decline can drastically change your retirement picture for the worse. Planning in this stage is a bit more challenging because your time horizon is unknown.

Retirement Money Phases Interact with Your Life

We go through different phases in our lives, and the same idea applies to our money. When you are young, placing a substantial portion of your investments in risk assets such as stocks, equity mutual funds, or ETFs makes sense as a way of accumulating wealth. However, as you get closer to retirement, you typically no longer have sufficient time to recover if the market were to decline for an extended period of time. Thus, a more conservative investing approach is called for when you are nearing the distribution phase of investing. Protecting your money, rather than growing it, becomes the top priority.

During my seminars and workshops on the topic of retirement, while on the topic of investing, I often use an example that highlights a more conservative, risk averse approach. For example, I'll ask the room to participate by raising their hands if they have ever been on a rollercoaster in their life; I then follow this question by asking if anyone has been on a rollercoaster in the past year. As you can probably guess, a "yes" answer to the first question is typically given by almost all of the seminar attendees, while only a few (and sometimes none) answer "yes" to the second question. Riding rollercoasters, like investing in volatile markets, is typically an endeavor better suited to a person's younger years. As we get older, we typically aim to reduce our risks, not increase them.

What does this mean for your retirement investments? It reinforces what I mentioned earlier about entering the distribution phase: you are likely to be less inclined to place a major portion of your investments in more volatile (riskier) investments the closer you get to retirement (and once you're retired). While these investments may offer higher returns, as your investment time horizon becomes shorter, there is less time to wait out potential market downturns. As a result, rollercoaster-type investments should make up a much smaller portion of your portfolio than they may have while in your younger years.

When you get close to or enter the distribution phase, your portfolio allocation should be changed to reflect your current circumstances. Instead of looking primarily for growth from your investments, the purpose will be to begin providing you with income in retirement. Whereas growth-oriented investments such as stocks, equity ETFs, and equity mutual funds predominated the accumulation phase, income-oriented investments such as bonds, fixed-income ETFs, fixed-income mutual funds, annuities, and income-producing real estate become more important during the distribution phase.

The primary goal when preparing for retirement should be to establish a lifetime income plan. Such a plan provides you with income from pensions, retirement plans, Social Security, annuities, and other income sources that aren't subject to the ups and downs of the stock market. Once you have adequately protected your money and created your lifetime income plan, you can focus on growing your remaining assets.

As you can imagine, accumulation and distribution phases lend themselves to very different strategies. Helping you navigate each of these phases requires a very different advisor experience and skill set. If you plan to work with an advisor as you prepare for retirement, seek an individual with a clearer understanding of the difference between these two phases. This is likely to produce the best results.

Changing How You View Your Money

As you can see, we need to change the way we view our money based on the phase we are currently in. We need to challenge our values and the way we view our dollars, as well as the purpose we attribute to each of those dollars. Changing your financial mindset for retirement may be difficult because once ideas about money become ingrained, they can be tough to change.

Since these adjustments represent a shift in the way we see money, one that can lead to a transition requiring big changes, many people decide to just stick with what they're already doing. Many people choose to take no action simply because they aren't sure which choices to make. Their attitude is, "if it's not broken, why fix it?" What they neglect to realize is what may not be broken *now* may end up being broken down the road, when it's needed the most.

CHAPTER 3

Retirement Challenges and Risks

As we have already touched upon, there are many challenges you're likely to face down the road to retirement. This chapter was written to provide education that can help you overcome these challenges and live the retirement lifestyle you want to live. Let's look at the various challenges and risks retirement brings:

Longevity Risk (Life Expectancy)

Longevity risk for an individual can be defined as the extent to which an individual's life span significantly exceeds his or her life expectancy. This is the risk of living longer than expected, and outliving your income and retirement plan, which is increasingly common in today's world. In retirement, longevity risk is one of the greatest risks, and in my opinion, a place where all risks start. The longer a retirement lasts, the greater the chances that other risks can become more magnified. The longer you live, the more the other risks matter,

50

and the increase in probability that they could become a concern.

Retirees don't know how long their retirement savings could last, and so they face a tradeoff between wanting to spend as much as possible without overdoing it, or tapping into their retirement funds aggressively and triggering financial insolvency. Increased longevity means more time to potentially get caught in a financial crisis, more time for inflation to compound and erode your savings, increased chances for expensive health issues to arise, and a greater risk you can run out of money through a lengthy retirement.

Nobody knows how long they will live, so longevity is the overarching risk, and one of the most daunting of risks all retirees face. The long-term financial cost of longevity is that either people can outlive their retirement savings, or alternatively, they could underspend their savings, leading to money being left over. People frequently underestimate their life expectancy, and thus, underestimate how much money they need throughout a lengthy retirement.

Emotional Decisions and Financial Advice

The biggest threats to your retirement are often based on the decisions you make and the external factors you cannot control. When it comes to market volatility, we often become our own worst enemy by letting emotions dictate our financial decisions. This may result in making choices that are ultimately wrong for us. An example of this would be taking financial advice or recommendations from a friend or colleague which may not be right for you and your personal situation because you feel like you're going to miss out on a profitable opportunity.

Unfortunately, it's very common for investors to do the wrong thing when their emotions are involved. Our core beliefs can often be a powerful force that leads us to something good; but at the same time, these beliefs can be the force that hurts us in the long run and can hold us back from opportunities. This is why we need a *plan* and *process* in place to monitor and ensure we stay on track, so we can avoid becoming our own worst enemy. We need the proper checks and balances.

One of the most common emotional investor mistakes I see is assuming market trends will continue for a long time. When the market is going up, people buy expecting that it can keep going up. However, when just the opposite happens, and the market starts going down, they often sell because they're expecting the downward trend to continue. In my experience, investors that act on emotion typically come late to the game. They miss out on much of the gains and partake in most of the losses. This, too, often results in the mistake of investors buying high and selling low. One benefit of hiring a financial advisor is that he or she can help you stay the course by navigating the pitfalls to making irrational decisions based on emotions.

Lack of Financial Education

Have you ever been to retirement school? Probably not. And why not? Because there is no such thing. But perhaps there should be. Here is the way I see it: you may be very good at what you do for a living (or what you did before retirement), but that doesn't necessarily mean you're good at planning for retirement. This is not to say you can't become very good at it, just that it may not come naturally. It can take significant time, effort, education, and training to successfully devise a sound retirement strategy.

When you walk through those doors to retirement, you should be able to answer three major questions:

1. What are you going to do with the rest of your life?
2. Do you have the financial resources to live the lifestyle you want to live, no matter how long your retirement may last?
3. Do you have a current risk management plan in place to protect your assets through a long retirement?

While this book is not meant to be a substitute for engaging in comprehensive retirement planning, it is intended to serve as an important tool in the process, and to provide you with a detailed account of a proactive approach to thinking about your retirement preparation. Look at this book as sort of a retirement school course, designed to teach some of the most important retirement planning and investing concepts, and how to apply them to enhance your chances of attaining your retirement goals and objectives. I know you may be thinking that you don't have the time, or crunching numbers just isn't your thing, but receiving an education on your retirement is one of the most important life courses you can take. As Chinese philosopher Lao Tzu said, "*The journey of a thousand miles starts with a single step.*" This book is one big step in your financial education.

Market Uncertainty

Uncertain markets and volatility are always and will always be present. Let me ask you this: where is the market headed? Do you know? Does anyone know? The truth is nobody knows for sure. Even the smartest financial minds and market pundits don't know. They all have opinions and hypotheses, but no one knows with absolute certainty which way the market is headed. You may have your own opinions about which direction the market is going to move. So, what if you're right? Great! But what if you're wrong?

If nobody knows for sure what the market will do on any given day, why gamble your hard-earned retirement dollars on the *hope* that the market does what you think it will? Always ask yourself, at any particular time you're invested in the market, "How much can I afford to lose?" If the markets go up, and you realize a 10 or 20 percent gain, would that dramatically change your retirement? What if the markets go down, and you take losses of that magnitude or more? What impact would that have on your financial plan?

There are many things we can't control that can affect our money. What are some of these outside forces? Things that seem to be happening more and more frequently, such as the potential of an increase in interest rates, a terrorist attack, an economic slump or crisis, political events, war, etc. What measures do you have in place to position your money for growth, while still having downside protection from market crashes?

Regarding market uncertainty, when it comes to investing, there's often a fine line between gambling and investing. And sometimes, it's hard to tell the two apart. Both strategies attempt to make money in the market. When is it gambling? And when is it investing? What's the difference?

In my opinion, investing is about attempting to achieve consistent long-term gains over time. As we get older and head into retirement, we still want to aim for reasonable returns with our money, but we also have to realize that time is not on our side. We can't afford to lose it all. On the flip side, gambling is more of a short-term mentality where you seek high returns, but can often encounter quite the opposite due to huge fluctuations and uncertainty.

An anecdote from a trip I took with a friend down to an event in Atlantic City can help illustrate this concept:

Both my friend and I set aside $200 to play blackjack. I'm a little more conservative than he is as a gambler. At the end of the first shoe (round), my stake was at $450. His was at $1,200. The reason being he was willing take more risk by riding his wins and "rolling the dice." At this point, he said to me, "Man, you are too conservative." I told him, "I don't want to lose it all." His reply was, "Rich, you've got to be in it to win it," which parallels the concept of being invested in the market aggressively at all times.

In the second shoe, my $450 turned into $650, and his $1,200 became $2,500 because he continued to take more risk, while I was more risk averse. At this point, I was a bit envious of his success, and I wondered if maybe I wasn't being aggressive enough, but I decided to stick with my strategy.

The next shoe came around, and it didn't go well, with my friend being even more aggressive than in the previous shoes. By the end of the third shoe, I was down to $400, and he was back down to the $200 he started with.

What lesson does this story teach us? Both of us sat down with $200, and I somehow walked away with more than my friend because I knew when enough was enough, while he kept pushing his luck. Every time I had a good hand, I pulled chips off the table, and I tucked them away. After a while, I was playing with house money, as my principle investment was secured in my pocket. My friend didn't know when to take chips off the table or when to walk away from a losing hand. In the end, he lost all his winnings, as well as the opportunity cost of the time spent at the table, which may have been better allocated elsewhere.

The moral of the story is when things are going well, it's really hard to walk away. It's difficult to change our frame of mind and think of preserving capital, while at the same time maintaining focus on making more of it. To overcome the danger of risking too much when things are going well, we need to change the way we look at money.

When things aren't going so well, don't compare yourself to others. After all, it's your money, not theirs. We never know where the top of the market is, and we never know where the bottom is; but based on our individual situation, we should have a goal set, and the mechanism in place to understand when we've hit our mark. We have to know when it's time to take some chips off the table, or in Wall Street terms, take some profits, without regret. For example, if you knew today that you had enough money to carry you throughout your retirement years, would you still take the same amount of risk?

When you enter retirement, you don't have time for the stock market to take your money and force you to wait for it to come back. You don't have time to ride out the ups and downs of the market. We all know over time the stock market tends to rise to higher levels. The problem is there are too many variables that affect the timing of exactly when this can happen. This is why younger investors are typically advised to invest a greater percentage of their assets in market-based investments, while older investors are advised to take a more cautious approach in search of safety and predictability.

Younger vs. Older investors

Do you feel older people should be invested the same way as younger people? Probably not. Why? As mentioned in the previous chapter, when you're younger and the market experiences significant corrections or crashes, you have time to wait for it to come back. But as you get older, and these corrections or crashes happen later in life, they can adversely affect even the best-devised retirement plans.

While accumulating assets during your younger years, it often makes sense to take a more growth-oriented approach to retirement investing. If started early enough, younger people have 30 to 50 years to allow their savings to grow. Because they have time to recover from a market downturn, investing more heavily in equity investments (ETFs, mutual funds, stocks) allows you to take advantage of the potentially higher returns that can be realized over long periods of time.

On the other hand, as we get older, we don't have time on our side. As we age, our investment focus should shift towards safety. As you head into retirement, your main earning years will be behind you. It's important to continue to keep your money working for you with the strategy of growth over time, but you also need to hedge and reduce risk as you get older to guard your retirement funds with as much principal safety as possible. That being said, a great exercise in figuring out the appropriate amount of risk you should have in your portfolio is to perform a risk assessment and examine how you respond to questions that directly measure your risk aversion. These questions help determine your risk tolerance, time horizons, income needs and objectives, and can typically offer some additional guidance as to how much risk you're actually taking. This can help determine how you should be investing your money.

Underestimating Investment Risk

We've all heard the old saying, "buy low and sell high." But who can say they have always bought low and sold high? In retirement, this lesson is magnified due to the lack of time on our side. What if you do the opposite? If you buy high and sell low in retirement, you simply don't have as much time to make up for such losses or mistakes as you did when you were younger. If you could always buy low and sell high, this wouldn't be an issue; but nobody knows with absolute certainty how to do this on a consistent basis. The one certainty about market returns is that it is completely random and *uncertain*. Predicting its ups and downs consistently is not possible, and anyone that claims otherwise should not be trusted.

The word "risk" means different things to different people. While some people look at risk as opportunity, most associate it with the potential of loss, or things being taken away. The good news is, not all risk is bad. The bad news is, too much risk in retirement can be devastating, and can bring with it unease and uncertainty. No matter how we view the word "risk," everybody still wants to feel secure with their retirement savings.

One of the most basic guiding principles of investing is to gradually reduce your risk over time as you get older. The principle is simple: the older you get, the shorter your time horizon. When you're older, you don't have the luxury of waiting for the market to bounce back after a big decline. The dilemma is figuring out exactly how safe you should be relative to your stage in life. For many years, the commonly cited *Rule of 100* has helped simplify asset allocation and risk. It states that your current age is proportional to the percentage of your retirement dollars dedicated to safe investments, protected from the ups and downs of the market, while the remainder of 100 minus your age represents the maximum percentage of money that can be at risk.

Below is an example that illustrates the recommended percentage mix between safe money and risk money for a 60-year old individual:

$$\frac{\begin{array}{l}100 \\ -60 \text{ (current age and safe money \%)}\end{array}}{40 \text{ (remainder and maximum risk money \%)}}$$

In theory, it's like a sliding scale, and every year as you get older, another percent should shift from the risk money bucket, to be placed into the safe money bucket, encouraging investors to slowly reduce risk over time. Many advisors agree with this concept in theory, however, the definition of what is considered "safe money" differs among advisors. While this guidance isn't perfect for everyone, it serves as a great starting point for examining your risk strategy in retirement, and should be re-examined each year.

I find that most people coming to see me for help with retirement are taking on far too much risk for their age. During these meetings together with the client, we add up their savings and investments, and we separate the two into safe money and risk money. Then, we compare the results to the Rule of 100 to see where they stand. Needless to say, quite often they are shocked at how much risk they are actually taking. I often have to be the one to help them realize they just can't afford to lose money at this point in their lives, and if a major correction were to happen this late in the game, it can change their retirement and lifestyle forever.

At Bravias Financial, the goal for our clients is to assume the smallest amount of risk as possible in retirement to reach their financial goals. Once we run a retirement analysis that shows our clients have the funds to carry them past age 100, we then shift our focus towards safety and protection.

When planning for retirement, it's vital to ask *why* you are doing what you're doing. Many investors blindly trust what their advisor or friends tell them they should do. This can often lead them to take an approach that may not be right for their particular situation. Every financial plan is different, and it should be customized to your particular goals, objectives and circumstances. In my opinion, you shouldn't have an advisor go ahead and invest your money unless you're sure of the financial situation you're in, the risk you're taking, and how the advisor's approach is likely to affect your retirement.

There Are No "Do-Overs"

Are you a golfer? I am, but not a very good one. In the game of golf, if you're playing with friends, and you take a bad shot, your friends will often allow you one *mulligan* per round. A mulligan is an extra stroke (second chance) allowed after a poor shot, usually after the first one went horribly wrong, and is not counted on the scorecard. Then, you get to take the shot again, like the previous swing never happened. Unfortunately, retirement is not like golf in this regard. In retirement, there are no mulligans or do-overs. You get one swing at it, and you've got to do it right. This is exactly why it's important that you have a solid plan in place, follow this plan, and make sound financial decisions along the way.

In retirement, the investment choices you make and their results, good or bad, are final. If your investments perform well, that's great. But if they perform poorly, you can't go back 5 or 10 years for another go-round. I often see people with a lackadaisical approach to planning for retirement. They even joke about going back to work if their investments falter in retirement. They act as though it's just that easy, when deep down inside they should know it's simply not a realistic option.

You either have enough money in retirement, or you don't. You either make the right moves with your money in retirement, or you don't. Navigating retirement and making the necessary adjustments along the way should not only provide peace of mind, but should also help ensure that retirement mulligans are never needed. The right financial advisor should be able to assist you with the essential education and knowledge you need to plan for retirement. If planned smart and done right, there should be no need for a second chance. Your golden years can be financially secure and enjoyable, as they should be.

Professional Advice (2nd Opinion)

The last retirement risk I want to address is the "do-it-yourself" mentality, or a lack of willingness to discuss your financial affairs with a professional. If you already have knowledge of the many investment products available, as well as their advantages and disadvantages, then I'm the first to suggest what I call, "self-managed retirement". However, in a fast-changing economy, I believe everyone should be updated and made aware of the latest products and retirement strategies that can potentially benefit them. I believe you should be given personalized guidance and not general, cookie-cutter advice. I believe most people should have a financial partner or coach to help guide them down the correct retirement planning path.

It's concerning that many people who approach me for financial assistance aren't even aware of the broad spectrum of products and services available to them. It's as if they've had financial blinders on their whole life. Most often, they are too busy to really dive in and become educated on their investment and retirement options. This is why my firm, Bravias Financial, leverages our experience and resources to offer a comprehensive platform that includes retirement strategy, investment management (through Bravias Capital Group, LLC), insurance planning, and income solutions. We also work in conjunction with specialists to offer estate planning and tax planning, among other services. The breadth of our offerings enables us to provide full-service solutions to meet all of our clients' financial needs.

It may be a good idea to get a 2nd opinion on your investments, which can provide a different perspective and other potential alternatives or solutions. Sometimes, the most important asset is a fresh set of eyes – a financial advisor can act as a sounding board by providing you with an independent second look. Every now and then, it can be helpful to take a step back and evaluate your current plan to make sure you still have confidence in it.

Choosing someone to help with your finances is an important decision, and it should be done with substantial care; the same kind of care you'd use when selecting anyone who is going to play an important role in your life. How do you choose your doctor? Your lawyer? Your accountant? Word of mouth is certainly one way of doing this, but you'd still want to take time and meet with that person to make sure the chemistry is there. Do you feel comfortable with this person? Do you feel they understand you? Do you trust them? If you can answer "yes" to these types of questions, I'd be inclined to take the next step in your research and meet with that individual.

CHAPTER 4

Holistic Planning – What is it and Why is it Important?

"In order to carry out a positive action, we must first develop a positive vision." - Dalai Lama

Before we jump into holistic planning, let's take a look at the word "holistic." The word comes from the Greek word *holos*, meaning entire, all, or whole. As this definition suggests, holism is the practice of paying attention to the whole of something, rather than attending to its individual parts. When providing financial planning services to my clients, I believe in taking a holistic view of a client's financial situation, then making recommendations that are tailored to their individual financial circumstances. This includes taking a comprehensive look at all of a client's financial needs: income planning, budgeting, taxes, investments, insurance, estate and retirement planning, or working with a client on a single financial issue, but within the context of their overall situation. This approach to achieving long-term financial well-being is superior, in my opinion, to an approach that focuses strictly on particular investment transactions without taking into account how they fit within a comprehensive financial plan.

My opinion is to find an advisor that looks at the whole picture, instead of just partial or transactional elements. For example, if you meet an advisor that just sells insurance, that's fine. But wouldn't it make more sense to work with an advisor that can look at the overall picture and quarterback a comprehensive game plan? Why would you want to go work with someone who doesn't take into account all aspects of the planning process? Imagine the frustration of putting together a big puzzle (your financial plan), and at the end, you are missing six or seven pieces. Compare that with going in from day one of the puzzle-assembling (planning) process knowing that everything it takes to complete the puzzle is in place. Which approach would you prefer?

Simply put, a holistic view of planning helps you understand how every financial decision you make can affect other areas of your life. It takes into consideration your financial situation, present and future, and demonstrates how everything fits together so you can clearly see where the process might take you. The goal is to simplify financial planning by enabling your financial advisor to make recommendations that take into consideration all facets of the big picture: your investments, your retirement goals, your time horizons, and a multitude of risks that may derail your plan. By viewing each financial decision as part of a whole, you can better understand the short and long-term impacts on your retirement goals, and best mitigate risk. I believe that when individuals pursue a holistic approach, they are far better equipped to face the future.

The holistic view of financial planning provides direction and purpose to your money. The personal and customized strategies created at the beginning of a client relationship help us to see both the wider view and the finer details. These strategies also produce an action plan, which serves as an ongoing benchmark used to keep us focused and on track.

Holistic Planning and Financial Analysis Software

The financial analysis software mentioned in Chapter 1 is an amazing resource for assisting an advisor when it comes to taking a look at the larger and potentially more complex issues related to your retirement plan. Funding a retirement plan requires discipline and commitment; for instance, doing things such as avoiding excessive expenditures and setting aside money from your paycheck to build up your assets.

However, the results of these efforts, a growing 401k/403b/TSP/457 statement or a swelling bank statement, as examples, typically don't provide the type of big picture view you can achieve through good financial planning tools.

The macro view provided by these programs gives you the opportunity to view your retirement savings accounts as a whole, which offers greater insight into how you're doing, and how you could be doing in the future as it relates to meeting your overall objectives. You can use this information to adjust your retirement account contributions or your asset allocations as necessary to improve the likelihood of achieving your retirement goals.

Financial planning software has made incredible advances over the years, so why not take advantage them? Tools like these can help you from a holistic planning perspective by providing visual aids such as graphs and charts, enabling you to envision the progress you're making towards your future retirement goals. By enabling you to view your retirement as a whole, planning software can help you understand how taking a holistic approach can improve your ability to prepare for retirement.

CHAPTER 5

Finding the Right Advisor

Have you ever wondered how to differentiate between a financial planner, financial advisor, and wealth manager? The issue is that these terms are often used interchangeably. So, who can you trust to help with your financial situation? When it comes to planning, there is much more than a title that comes into play. Regardless of what's on their business card, I believe it's important to work with an advisor that takes a holistic approach to financial planning.

Let me tell you why I feel this way. Just like our everyday lives, there are many different moving parts that need to work within the framework of your financial plan – from insurance and healthcare planning to investment management, income planning, estate planning and tax planning. However, not every advisor is equipped to, or interested in, taking into account all of the pieces of the financial puzzle. A holistic advisor not only considers, but plans for, all of the various components that make up your financial plan, even if they need assistance from outside their scope of expertise. The end result: a true understanding of your complete financial picture, along with advice and consideration of how each piece affects the others.

When all is said, it's prudent to work with an advisor that really digs through the weeds and gets to know you, your particular financial situation, where you want to be down the road, what your priorities are, and shares your long-term vision for a happy and stress-free retirement. In my opinion, your first appointment with an advisor should be at least an hour, if not longer, so that there's enough time for you to get to know each other, and you are able to provide the advisor with a complete picture of your financial situation.

The purpose of this first meeting is to take comprehensive inventory and obtain a detailed "lay of the land". This includes gathering information such as the following:

- Relevant details about you and your family
- Employment info
- Cash flow needs
- Risk tolerance
- Goals and objectives
- Insurance coverage
- Assets
- Retirement time horizon
- Monthly expenses

In other words, if an advisor takes the time to truly understand you, then that's a positive sign, and you should feel a little more comfortable that they aren't just looking for a quick sale. Your advisor should comprehend the whole picture so they can provide better overall advice.

The Manner in Which Financial Advice is Given

Suitability standard vs. Fiduciary standard

Simply put, the *suitability standard* requires that a broker (registered representative) make recommendations that are suitable based on a client's personal situation. The standard does not require the advice to be in the client's best interest. The suitability standard is enforced through a self-regulatory organization called the Financial Industry Regulatory Authority (FINRA).

On the other hand, the *fiduciary standard* requires advisors to put their clients' interests first and foremost. By being held to the fiduciary standard, my role requires me to provide recommendations independent of outside influences, and I am legally obligated to do so. The fiduciary standard is adhered to by Registered Investment Advisors (RIA's) and enforced by the Securities and Exchange Commission (SEC) or the individual state where the RIA is registered.

My firm, Bravias Financial, is an independent financial planning firm, meaning that we work for our clients and solely represent them, rather than any particular company. This independence, in my opinion, is vital to delivering objective advice. As an independent firm, we are not owned by a bank, insurance company, or another investment firm. We have the freedom to choose the companies we work with, and the products we recommend to our clients. This allows us to provide unbiased, comprehensive advice in the best interest of each individual client.

How to Find the Right Advisor

Choosing the right financial advisor to help you plan your family's future is a big decision. Most people consider a variety of different factors when interviewing potential financial advisors. There are several important questions to ask any advisor before making a decision to work with him or her.

Just as you are free to choose the financial advisor you believe is best suited to help you meet your goals and objectives while providing you the level of service and support you need, independent financial planning firms benefit from a similar freedom of choice, with the ability to recommend what's best for our clients with an "open architecture" approach. This means we can access a wide array of financial products, enabling us to honor our fiduciary duty by putting the clients' needs above all else. Isn't that the way it should be? I suggest you find out what standard of advice your current (or

73

PLAN SMART, RETIRE RIGHT

prospective) advisor provides and use this information to make the decision that's best for you and your goals.

Many financial firms (not all) offer proprietary or "affiliate" products. This means the firms typically receive more revenue, and the advisor often receives extra incentives or compensation, to recommend or promote certain products above others. This can potentially create a conflict of interest. If you were them, what would you do? This is why it's important to conduct your research and due diligence, and ask the right questions, regardless of which direction you decide to go. Knowledge is power!

Here are the questions I'd want answered before I entrusted my financial future to anyone:

1. Are you held to the suitability standard or fiduciary standard?

As I mentioned above, those held to the fiduciary standard are legally obligated to put their clients' interests first, whereas those acting as non-fiduciaries can offer advice that may not necessarily be in your best interest. Only advisors bound by fiduciary duty are required to put your needs first. If they are not held to the fiduciary standard, then keep in mind they are likely a broker or agent, and not *legally* obligated to put your needs first. As the name suggests, the "suitability standard" requires only that the broker have a reasonable belief that any recommendations made are suitable for the client in terms of their financial needs, objectives, and unique circumstances.

It may be wise to work with a Registered Investment Adviser (RIA), an Investment Advisor Representative (IAR) or anyone else who is held to the fiduciary standard. By definition, they are held to a higher degree of accountability than most brokers (registered representatives), and it's my belief that you'll often find them to be the more knowledgeable when it comes to investment management. Not to say that there aren't many qualified people in this industry; I just think it's important to understand the manner of advice you'll be receiving, and make sure it's a good fit for you and your particular situation.

2. How do you get compensated?

This is probably one of the most important questions to ask, and for multiple reasons. In many cases, an advisor should be up front and volunteer this information, which is typically a good sign. Are they commission-based? Are they fee-based? Are they both? If they are not able to effectively communicate this information, it should raise some concern. If they are fee-based, ask follow-up questions regarding how these fees are assessed – assets under management, flat fees, planning fees, etc. It's important to understand how the person you trust with your financial future is compensated to ensure his or her interests are aligned with your retirement goals.

Secondly, it's not only important to learn how an advisor is compensated, it's also important to understand the scope of services you will be receiving for that compensation. Will their commission or fee include other additional services, or is everything a-la-carte? I'm not saying there is a right or wrong approach, but if you're considering having a financial advisor manage a large percentage of your money, you should know exactly what they're doing for you. Think of it this way: if you went to a nice restaurant, and the menu didn't have any pricing on it, you'd probably ask what certain items cost and what comes with them, wouldn't you?

Once you understand how the financial advisor is compensated, and what services they provide for that compensation, you now have the knowledge required to make an informed decision as to whether or not your needs are going to be met.

3. Does your firm offer proprietary products or have selling/affiliate/partnership/joint venture agreements with other companies?

If the answer is yes, no matter what capacity they are held to, there is the possibility they may steer you towards financial products which are good for them and/or their firm, but may not necessarily equate to the best choice of products for you. They are incentivized and sometimes even required to recommend these products – and they typically receive higher commissions for selling them. Ideally, your advisor should be completely unbiased when it comes to investment advice. Especially when your retirement is on the line.

What does this mean for you? Most independent financial advisors have no products to push or corporate goals to meet. This freedom gives us the ability to stay laser-focused on our core purpose: serving clients with independent and unbiased advice. Clients can rest assured the advice we offer and every action we take are tailored towards their individual needs and goals.

4. When I become a client, where are my investment assets held?

This question is important because, in my opinion, you'd sleep better at night knowing your assets are held at a third-party custodian or institution like TD Ameritrade, Schwab, Pershing, Fidelity, etc. This arrangement is critical and ultimately protects you from having your money at risk of a scam or con, like the Bernie Madoff scandal. Bernie Madoff's failure to use an independent custodian enabled him to defraud investors for many years. A third-party custodian provides periodic (monthly or quarterly) statements independent of any reports provided by the advisor. This creates a critical barrier between your funds and any advisor. If a financial advisor tells you that you don't need this type of arrangement, end the meeting and leave immediately. This should be a deal-killer and raise many red flags.

5. What is your investment philosophy or approach?

I like this question because you get to catch a glimpse of where the advisor's planning is going to take you. A disciplined approach to financial planning should be the foundation for a sound investment process that considers all relevant planning activities and breaks them down into doable steps. Having this sneak peek into the way they manage funds can help you decide if it makes sense to you and fits into what you are looking to achieve.

Ultimately, are you comfortable with this person? There are many different investment philosophies and methodologies, and each advisor may have good reasons for believing in his or hers. The truth is, I think it's important that their methods are purposeful and articulated in advance, so you are not making emotional decisions during times of heightened market volatility. It is crucial that you fully understand your financial advisor's investment approach and agree with how he or she will execute it.

Every financial advisor has their own specific approach to planning and investing. Some advisors prefer trying to time the market, versus a buy-and-hold investment approach. Others may seek to gain higher returns by making riskier investments. Your goals and risk tolerance need to align with the advisor's philosophy. Anyone investing money generally does so in the hope of growing it faster than inflation.

Some traditional investment managers not only want to generate a profitable return, they also aim to "beat the market" by attempting to time the market and predict the future, which I don't recommend, nor condone. Some investment companies offer one-size-fits-all investment management solutions that only take into account your age and income.

Make it a top priority to understand the strategy your advisor uses and verify that it's a strategy you are comfortable with.

6. Can you describe your client service model?

The answer to this question can tell you a lot about the client experience, what his or her priorities are with regards to serving clients, and how often the advisor plans on reviewing your investments. As one would imagine, these are important items to discuss upfront. Most people who work with an advisor assume that the advisor will pay close attention to their money, make adjustments as needed, and stay abreast of new information that could possibly put them in a better overall situation. However, your advisor may have a vastly different opinion of what constitutes client service, and if you don't ask, you won't know for sure.

As you can see, finding a financial advisor that is right for you is an important process, and it shouldn't be taken lightly. A good financial advisor is there to prevent you from making decisions that may have a negative, unintended impact on you or your financial situation. Who wouldn't love having a financial coach to keep you on track towards achieving your financial goals? That should be his or her primary mission in serving his or her clients.

As with any working relationship, it's a good idea to interview advisors until you find the one best suited to you and your financial goals. Do you feel the advisor understands you and your specific circumstances? Since you're entrusting your financial well-being to someone, and you are about to enter into a relationship that will hopefully last a long time, you should get to know them and their financial planning & investing philosophy up front. If you have any reservations, move on. There are plenty of qualified advisors out there, and you shouldn't settle for one if you are less than 100% confident in your decision.

CHAPTER 6

Five Retirement Checkpoints

"Most people don't plan to fail, they fail to plan."
– John Beckley

One of the most frequently asked questions I receive from clients is, "Am I on the right path to retirement?" As you can imagine, this is a difficult question to answer because the road to retirement is not the same for everyone. To keep you on track when it comes to planning for your retirement, it's important to address these five key checkpoints along the way:

1. Have a well thought-out, written retirement plan

Wouldn't it be nice if there were something you could do to help prepare for retirement which allowed you to feel more secure in your future? There is something you can do, and it's

81

called putting your retirement plan in writing. A 2016 LIMRA Secure Retirement Institute study (*www.limra.com/secureretirementinstitute*) found that pre-retirees and retirees (ages 55-75 with financial assets of $100,000+) who have formal written retirement plans, are more likely to feel confident they're saving enough for retirement, and more than twice as likely to feel very prepared for retirement, than those without a written plan.

This research demonstrates that creating a formal, written retirement plan involving a comprehensive discussion about goals, asset management and risk mitigation, often leads to better outcomes in retirement. So, what does that study teach us? Don't "wing it" by hoping everything will turn out for the best when it comes to your retirement. If you don't have something tangible you can look at and refer to, then face it, you're winging it. Writing down your plan makes it more concrete. It enables you to visualize the results associated with different savings and investment approaches. Think of a written plan as assembly instructions. When you purchase something that needs to be put together, the included instructions provide the steps you need to follow in order to properly and successfully assemble it. Financial planning is no different, and having step-by-step instructions to follow can help hold the plan together and keep you on track.

When attempting to achieve goals of any type, especially complex or multi-part goals, having a written plan of some sort is always advisable. Given the importance of planning for retirement, putting your plans into some sort of written context is essential. This can take the form of a list of goals and the steps necessary to achieve those goals, or a more formal financial plan with charts that graphically display how your money needs to grow in order to meet your objectives. Having a written plan allows you and your advisor to make adjustments together, if and when the need should arise.

2. Create a reliable lifetime income foundation

Maximizing retirement income and making sure you fill any income gaps throughout retirement are probably the most crucial parts of the planning process. When you reach retirement, your income sources should be as reliable as possible, especially if you want to maintain the same lifestyle you had during your working years. This means investments such as annuities, bonds, or real estate, which can provide stable income, should typically be favored over stock market investments for income purposes. In many cases, pension and Social Security payments may not be enough to fund the full amount of income necessary. Planning ahead is essential to fill these retirement income gaps.

Unfortunately, in many cases, I speak with people who wait until they are near retirement before taking steps to ensure they can fill these income gaps. To avoid this, you should plan as far ahead as possible, and there's no better day than today. This can help improve your chances of creating enough cash flow from other sources to further supplement your income from pension plans and Social Security in retirement. There are different strategies you can deploy regarding your pension, Social Security, and other income-producing assets where you can maximize the returns by strategizing the most opportune time and order in which to withdraw them.

Developing a retirement income strategy can help to ensure you are protecting yourself against key retirement risks; making sure you don't outlive your money, keeping up with inflation, and protecting your monthly cash flow from any outside forces. Essentially, the key is that you are optimizing your investments and other income sources to the best of your ability. In later chapters, I will discuss ways you can create a reliable income for yourself.

3. Build a sound investment strategy

In my experience, many investors struggle with managing investment risk. Once we retire, the goal for most of us is less about how to grow our nest egg as big as possible, and more about ensuring that the money we've accumulated can carry us through a long retirement. Your investment portfolio should be fully diversified with the aim of reducing risk in retirement. It should consider your risk tolerance, retirement income needs, life expectancy, and most importantly, your age. Things change in life and in the markets, and your investments should be adjusted accordingly. In addition to being diversified, your portfolio should also be actively managed to a certain degree, so that it's responsive to changes in the market and in your life. Don't settle for a "set it and forget it" approach.

One change that many investors encounter is the need for a reduction in their risk tolerance over time. When entering retirement, your ability to take risks declines for two reasons. First, you lack the flexibility of going back to work or taking on another job to make up for any investment losses you may suffer. Second, you have less time to make up for losses. As a result, your investment plan should incorporate steps to reduce the risk in your portfolio as you get close to and enter into retirement. A reduction of risk tolerance can often manifest itself through proper diversification and asset allocation. In Chapter 10, I will show you ways to build a solid investment plan.

4. Have a risk management strategy plan in place

Even the best retirement plans can be vulnerable and subject to the unexpected, unpredictable, or unknown. While you can't control all risks, you can certainly address them in your planning process.

Risk management is a key component to any sound investment strategy and comprehensive retirement plan. Managing the risks that retirees face is critical to the success of their retirement plan. From longevity risks, market risks, and inflation risks, to health risks and beyond, there are many potential "what if's" one must think through and plan for in retirement. It can seem like quite a daunting task to address all these issues as you shift from your accumulation phase to distribution in your retirement years.

While meeting with clients, one of my primary goals is to show them how to take their key retirement risks off the table. Having a risk management strategy in place enables them to examine their vulnerabilities and plan for the unexpected. The concept of risk management and the steps needed to build a plan for dealing with threats to retirement are covered more deeply in Chapter 7.

5. Have a long-term care plan

What will happen *when* you need long-term care? You've worked hard your whole life and saved for retirement, but sometimes the unforeseen happens. What if you develop an illness or cognitive disorder, fall victim to an accident, or become seriously hurt for an extended period of time? What if no one else is available to provide the care you need? Who would do it? And how would you pay for it? Enter Long-term care (LTC) insurance. Long-term care is assistance needed due to a loss of functional capacity caused by an illness, injury, or severe cognitive disorder. LTC insurance can provide you the high-quality care you need in the setting of your choice.

One of the biggest threats to anyone's savings and retirement funds is entering into a long-term care situation. In a recent study (*Medicare & You, 2015)*, 70% of people over age 65, and 97% of those over 85, could require long-term care at some point in their lives. Long-term care, whether nursing home care, skilled care, or home health care, depletes your wealth and can be more financially devastating to your retirement than the worst stock market correction. In the event of a long-term care situation, assets intended for retirement are often used to cover these expenses. For most people, the default long-term care plan would be to self-fund any expenses until all assets are depleted, and then to transition into Medicaid (a government welfare program). Furthermore, a common misconception is that Medicare pays for long-term care; generally speaking, it doesn't.

As you would probably expect, long-term care costs are quite high. According to a 2016 survey by *Care Scout*, the average cost of care in New Jersey (for example) ranges from home health care at approximately $52,000 per year to as high as $130,000 per year for private nursing home care, per person. With rising healthcare costs and inflation, these numbers increase on an annual basis. Since LTC insurance is based on health and age, the cost of delaying your purchase of LTC insurance could exceed 8-10% in premium increases per year. Planning on how to manage these expenses is an essential part of retirement planning. Unfortunately, it's often overlooked. No retirement plan is complete without proper consideration of how to integrate funding for potential long-term care needs.

It is my opinion that everyone should consider some type of LTC contingency plan, and I personally feel that any financial advisor not discussing this potential risk to your retirement plan is not doing their job. It's one thing to not want it, to not be able to afford it, or to be approved for it – but it's another thing to not be educated about it, or the devastating affects a long-term care situation can have on your financial plan. There are many different types of LTC insurance policies out there, from traditional policies to asset-based policies, all with different features and add-ons (riders). It's important to sit down with a knowledgeable insurance agent to customize a plan that works for your budget and needs.

LTC insurance is one of the best financial tools available to protect your assets, maintain your independence, and prevent you from becoming a financial or emotional burden on family members. In our opinion, no retirement plan is complete without a proper consideration of how to integrate funding for potential long-term care needs.

We live in a time where saving and planning for retirement is *your* responsibility, and you need to take ownership of what you do, or don't do, to properly plan. The five checkpoints are about not only making sure you have a plan in place and reducing as many risks in retirement as possible to make your money last, but also about steps you can take at any age to ensure you've addressed the most important overarching issues that can dramatically shape what your retirement looks like.

CHAPTER 7

Investment Risk Management

"Rule #1: Never lose money. Rule #2: Never forget Rule #1."
– Warren Buffet

There are many unknowns in life that can affect how we create and build wealth. As mentioned previously, risk management is about planning for the things we know can or will happen, as well as planning for things we hope never do. However, *investment* risk management is about anticipating waves of market volatility and protecting investments from adverse market events.

By ignoring that you have financial risks in retirement, you've already doomed yourself and your money. The answer isn't to bury your head in the sand, cross your fingers, and hope you've made the right decisions. There is tremendous peace of mind that comes from knowing you've taken the necessary steps to cover your bases and address things that are out of your control. When you properly plan, you can prepare for surprises, as opposed to subjecting your retirement to the winds of unpredictability.

To successfully navigate this ever-changing world, you must continue to have confidence in the process and strategies you've put in place. In a time where longevity, inflation, market uncertainty, rising healthcare costs, and a depleting Social Security fund are all in play, it may make sense to seek the advice of someone who has a deep understanding of investment risk management and asset protection.

The risks to your retirement plan are many and varied. Generally speaking, the main investment risks you are likely to face when planning for retirement fall into the following categories:

Market risk

Market volatility and fluctuations, both upwards and downwards, are common features in all markets. The risk of a significant downward trend occurring in the market is known as *market risk*. As we all know, market volatility is inevitable and unpredictable. Throughout life, investors are almost certain to experience years of volatility, market corrections or crashes, and negative portfolio performance at some point or another. If this volatility happens to correspond with your retirement, it may dramatically affect your savings and income. History has shown us that equities perform well over the long-term. However, short-term market shocks and potential uncertainty can cause retirement portfolios to substantially fluctuate.

One of the major risks facing investors is the impact of multiple bad years of investment performance. This can be an increasingly significant problem as you approach retirement since liquidating investments for income in a down market can amplify the effect of negative returns on your savings. While nobody can consistently and accurately predict the timing of market declines or how long they'll last, there are ways to better protect your retirement funds from market losses, and prevent those markets from affecting your retirement income in sustained periods of decline. I will tackle these in the next several chapters.

Interest rate risk

In a low interest rate environment, *yield* can be challenging to find. The term yield is used to describe the annual return on your investments as a percentage of your original investment, usually from either:

- Dividend payments from a stock, ETF or mutual fund
- Interest payments from a bond

In general, lower interest rates weaken retirement income and rates on *safer* vehicles we typically use to stash money (savings accounts, CD's, etc.). As a result, individuals either need to save more, or take additional risk, in order to accumulate the needed retirement funds. When rates are low, we often tend to leverage our safe (has-to-be-there-for-retirement) money and take more risk than we should in an effort to chase returns.

When interest rates rise, the value of fixed income investments such as bonds decline in value. This is no big deal if you plan to hold a bond until it matures, but can become worrisome should you need to sell it during a period when interest rates are rising. Of course, investors can benefit by receiving more income on their investments when interest rates increase, so this risk is more relevant to retirees planning to sell their bond holdings, or with heavy exposure to the stock market, which can react badly in times of rising interest rates.

Inflation risk

Inflation, sometimes referred to as *the invisible tax*, is the increase of the cost of goods and services from year to year. *Inflation risk* is the possibility that the value of assets or income can decrease as the purchasing power of a currency shrinks. Inflation causes money to decrease in value at some rate and does so whether the money is invested or not. In simpler terms, it often makes sense to invest conservatively in retirement without being too conservative, or else we run the risk of eroding our portfolios over time with inflation. Inflation is one of the biggest retirement challenges I see impacting a long retirement, and most people don't plan for it.

Many retirees may not realize the full extent of their exposure to inflation over time. For retirees living on a fixed income, rising prices can slowly erode their purchasing power, as the cost of goods and services become more expensive. Personally, I feel only a small portion of retirees will be able to live comfortably on a fixed income for the rest of their lives, especially if they live longer than expected. At some point, inflation can exceed the income they're counting on to cover monthly expenses; then, retirees would be forced to start withdrawing from their long-term investments and/or liquidating assets to fill the income gaps inflation has created. These are the same investments that need to last as long as the retiree is alive. This can turn out to be difficult to achieve if the purchasing power is declining.

Income risk

Sustaining lifetime income throughout retirement is a critical portfolio objective for most people, and for me. Our retirement typically depends on the amount of funds we are able to set aside for retirement income purposes. If those savings are reduced or depleted, either due to job loss, a career change, market correction, a healthcare issue, or other factors, it can negatively impact even the best retirement plans. For instance, if you are forced to go on long-term disability because of an accident or an unexpected illness, the reduction in income may result in a hit to your long-term income projections and cash flow.

It's important to have certain monies earmarked for (or easily converted to) retirement income – and these monies need to provide a reliable source of income to supplement any retirement income gaps. As you can imagine, there are many strategies that can be put into place to help manage retirement income risk, and a strong understanding of these strategies should help protect retirement dollars when uncertainty strikes. If you want to plan for pension-like income in retirement, it may make sense to utilize the services of a financial advisor. Just be sure to choose one that has a full understanding of the different types of income annuities and income risk management strategies available.

Circumstantial (unexpected) risk

Even the most carefully crafted retirement plans can be thwarted by unexpected events. For instance, your adult children may need you for financial help and/or to move back home while you're retired. You could potentially get sued, divorced, taxes could be raised dramatically where you live, or another assortment of life's twists and turns could derail your plan.

Let's take a look at another example: an unfortunate circumstance that one of my close friends had to deal with last year when his home was damaged in a flood. You might think this type of damage would have been covered under his homeowner's policy, but with some policies, this is not the case. In addition, most policies in areas where flooding is more likely to occur do not cover the contents of your home. My friend was responsible for all repair expenses relating to the water damage of his home, in addition to replacement costs for clothing, furniture, electronics, and family heirlooms. Without proper planning, having to foot the bill for this type of unexpected event can deal a significant blow to your retirement funds.

The risks of unexpected circumstances don't necessarily have to take the form of catastrophic events of one type or the other. For example, if you have priced the cost of college education recently, you know that depending on the institution selected, the price tag can be substantially different. So, if you've budgeted, let's say, $30,000 a year in college costs, only to find that your child wants to attend a college that costs $60,000 a year, such a disparity has the potential to wreak havoc on your carefully-planned retirement savings.

While this type of risk can never be totally eliminated, planning to have an emergency savings fund in retirement can help you deal with such issues should they arise. As I always say, better to be prepared than surprised.

"I am more concerned with the return of my money than the return on my money." - Will Rogers

---

Proper Planning via Risk Management

In planning and preparing for retirement, scaling back your aggressive investing is important because a catastrophic market event could crush your retirement. For example, consider the most recent market calamity from 2007 to 2009. If you happened to retire during those years, and you were heavily invested in stocks, corporate bonds and mutual funds, your retirement may have sustained huge losses, and probably looked much different than you expected.

Proper risk management is sort of like having retirement insurance, whereas you can place a safety net around your money. For example, why do we have insurance? Homeowner's insurance, auto insurance, health insurance, and life insurance are all intended to protect the things that are important to us from loss, and from the unexpected. It amazes me to see that people don't think about protecting their biggest investment assets, or the things most important to them. To use a baseball analogy, retirement planning should be less about trying to hit homeruns, and more about hitting singles, earning a reasonable rate of return with as much principal protection as possible, so you don't strike out.

Let's look at this through a different lens. If you've ever gone bowling, depending on your skill set and age, you may have had a bowling alley employee put up guardrails to stop your ball from going into the gutter. With the guardrails up, no matter how badly you play, you still have a chance of knocking down pins. There is no chance of guttering every ball or scoring a "0". Properly diversifying your savings and investments among all available asset classes is like putting up guardrails around your retirement.

We can't control what the market does with our money, but we can certainly control what *we* do with our money. At the end of the day, it's your responsibility to take control of your retirement plan. With careful planning, you don't need to worry or stress about the future and the things you can't control. Instead, focus on things you *can* control. If done correctly, you can build what I often refer to as a *bulletproof financial plan*, where no matter what happens around you, your income and assets are protected. When such a plan is executed correctly, your risk of running out of money in retirement is significantly reduced.

"My #1 rule on investing in retirement: You don't need to make huge rates of returns on your money for it to last. You just need to avoid huge losses."
- Richard Zeitz

A well thought-out and strategic plan with a focus on risk management can help protect against or minimize downside, while setting you up for a long and stress-free retirement, where fear and uncertainty have no place. How would it make you feel to know that you can't outlive your money in retirement? How would it make you feel to know that you have retirement security, regardless of what happens in the stock market or with other outside variables?

When I think of what successful financial planning means to me, it's all about putting a plan in place that brings certainty, even in uncertain times. We can't possibly know without any doubt what the market will do on a daily basis, or what can happen with other factors (the cost of living, taxes, etc.) that can affect our retirement. Every precaution must be taken to make sure our retirement can withstand the potential pitfalls that may come our way. The easiest way to enjoy a stress-free retirement savings plan is to place a "force field" around it.

Believing in Murphy's Law: "Whatever can possibly go wrong, will go wrong," is the first step in determining risk and preparing for it. This simply means, don't rely only on a best-case scenario when it comes to planning for retirement; you must consider all potential outcomes, and prepare for worst-case scenarios as well. Design your retirement plan to respond accordingly.

A person has four choices when dealing with risk:

1. *Accept the risk.*

   Risk acceptance involves accepting what is meant to be, so to speak. It's essentially rolling the dice with the goal of weathering the impact of an event. This option is often chosen by those who consider the cost of risk transfer or reduction to be excessive or unnecessary. I feel that risk acceptance is a dangerous strategy, as your overall plan becomes vulnerable in the event an unexpected incident occurs.

2. *Avoid the risk.*

   Obviously, one of the easiest ways to mitigate risk is to put a stop to anything that might put your financial plan in jeopardy. However, it's important to remember that not all risk can be avoided. As the saying goes, life happens, and it's often not a realistic option for many people to completely avoid all risk.

3. ***Reduce the risk.***

Another risk management technique is reduction - essentially, this means taking the necessary steps required to minimize the potential that something will happen. Risk reduction strategies need to be weighed in terms of their potential return on investment. If the cost of risk reduction outweighs the potential cost of an incident occurring, you need to decide whether it's really worth it.

4. ***Transfer the risk.***

I feel one of the best methods of risk management is to transfer that risk to another party. Examples of this strategy in action are life insurance or long-term care insurance. Risk transfer is a realistic approach to risk management, as it assumes that sometimes incidents happen, yet ensures that your overall plan can cope with the impact of that eventuality.

When it comes to planning for retirement, I employ a *hope for the best, and plan for the worst* approach with my clients, not the other way around. Rather than counting on the best-case scenario, I believe you need to plan for the unexpected. We can never fully anticipate or prepare for every scenario – the future is too unpredictable. Instead of avoiding all risks (which is impossible), learn proven ways to manage them.

An important step to take in order to better understand and plan for the risks to your retirement is to sit down with a financial advisor to examine your individual situation and ask the following questions. You may find they aren't always easy to answer.

1. What risks do we face, and where might they come from?
2. Which investment assets are exposed?
3. What financial burden do these risks place on our money and retirement?
4. How can we better invest to reduce risk or safeguard our assets?

Retirement Risk Management Model

As stated in earlier chapters, I believe planning for retirement doesn't have to be overly difficult. When meeting a potential client for the first time, I walk them through our Retirement Risk Management Model, which takes a more manageable approach to financial planning with a clear breakdown of identified steps. The purpose of this model is to show the client where our planning focus lies, and the steps needed to build a plan that can guide them to a worry-free retirement on their terms.

This process affords us the ability to examine income and expenses throughout retirement, potential gaps in protection and risk exposure, savings, investments, and what would be left to beneficiaries. With all of this in mind, I can better understand a client's unique situation, and provide them with customized solutions that can be easily understood and implemented.

Retirement Risk Management Model

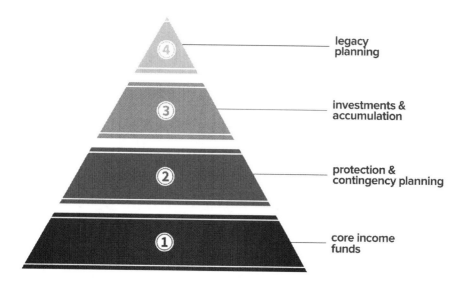

"Invincibility lies in the defense." – Sun Tzu

Let's define each level of my Retirement Risk Management Model, starting with the base, and working our way up:

Core Income Funds

Core income is the foundation of your financial plan, covering all of your essentials and "must-haves". These guaranteed income sources create lifetime monthly cash flow that is protected from fluctuations, corrections, or recessions in the markets, and continues, no matter what. They can consist of pensions, Social Security, income annuities, real estate, and high-quality bonds such as those issued by the U.S. Government. In Chapter 9, I will explain "green money" and core income planning in more detail to show you how to go about constructing additional lifetime income streams to generate more cash flow in retirement.

Contingency and Protection Planning

This is the level where you address things that could derail your retirement plan – such as an accident, disability, or long-term care situation. Planning of this type helps you think about and prepare for the unexpected.

By utilizing insurance products and other contingency planning strategies, you can better protect everything and everyone important to you from an unintended disaster. Taking the necessary protection and proper precautions enable you to secure your core income and ensure you and your loved ones are covered in an event the unexpected occurs.

Investments and Accumulation

This is the level at which you utilize various methods to grow and protect your wealth over time. An optimal and sustainable investment strategy takes into account both capital growth and wealth preservation. Offensive and defensive strategies in investing can be combined to foster the growth of wealth for retirement using a diversified approach that helps protect your assets from being too exposed to any one stock, market, or asset class.

Most people believe investing is risky. I believe investing can be risky if you lack the financial education or guidance to invest prudently. Ultimately, investing is one of the keys to financial freedom. If you take a measured and calculated approach to managing your investment portfolio, investing can help you live the life you want to live in retirement; whereas taking a reckless approach can certainly have the opposite effect.

Even though you spend all your working years accumulating wealth, many people spend just as many years in retirement. Proper planning and investment in retirement is critical, and learning how to invest correctly means learning how to make your money work for you. One of the biggest challenges in investing, especially in retirement, is making sure you have some type of risk management in place to protect your money in the case of crashes or market corrections. Make sure you don't overemphasize growth in your retirement planning at the cost of exposing your quality of life in retirement to the whims of the market. I'll discuss investment planning and accumulation later in Chapter 10.

Legacy Planning

Contrary to what many believe, legacy planning is not just a financial concept for the wealthy. In its simplest form, legacy planning has to do with strategies you can implement to ensure you maximize what you'll leave to your kids, your beneficiaries, your favorite charity, etc. Legacy planning helps direct where your money goes when you pass away. Often, this can be accomplished with a carefully curated selection of insurance and financial products. Further, there are basic components to estate planning you should consider as well, such as a will, power of attorney, and health care proxy, to name a few. An attorney, or more specifically an estate attorney, can assist with properly preparing these items for you.

Working with an Advisor to Help Manage Risk

When it comes to retirement planning and managing risks throughout, there are many benefits to working with a financial advisor; and the later we reach in life, the more these benefits are exponentially magnified. The right financial advisor could help you better identify and understand your retirement risks in all aspects of your financial life, and help develop personalized strategies to keep your goals and objectives in line.

CHAPTER 8

The "Purpose" of Your Money

In Chapter 2, we discussed accumulation vs. distribution, and the purpose of our money in these two distinct phases. I believe every dollar we have has a purpose, and understanding that purpose can help make sense of the money we have accumulated. When drawing up your retirement investment plan, building an integrated retirement income foundation is the key, and should help you create a more efficient overall retirement portfolio. You need a plan that can provide a stable source of reliable retirement income you can't outlive. Your pension and Social Security may not provide sufficient income for this purpose, which is where your retirement investments come into play. I always recommend that my clients take inventory of their investments and savings, and split them into one of two categories based on their overall retirement goal:

1. ***Green "income" money*** - Making sure you generate enough monthly positive cash flow to live the lifestyle you want.

2. ***Red "risk" money*** - Making sure you optimize the rest of your money while consistently managing investment risk.

THE PURPOSE OF YOUR MONEY

GREEN
"INCOME"
MONEY

PURPOSE:

LIFETIME INCOME

RED
"RISK"
MONEY

PURPOSE:

LONG-TERM GROWTH

The difference between the amount of income you need in retirement to cover your expenses and maintain your lifestyle, and the amount supplied by reliable income sources such as a pension and Social Security, is what is commonly referred to as the retirement *income gap*. This gap is my first focus when it comes to determining what my clients need to secure for retirement. Some people rely on their long-term retirement investments, *red "risk" money*, to fill this gap once they retire. However, this approach can be dangerous because without the use of good planning software and sound strategy, it's often difficult to determine how much of these funds you should use each year (depending on market gains or declines) while maintaining the discipline necessary to consistently allocate the correct amounts.

If it isn't clear exactly how much income you should take from your investments and savings to fill the income gap in retirement, it may be tempting to take more than you should. If you consistently take more than sustainable amounts out of your investment funds, there may come a time when these funds are exhausted or are no longer able to generate enough money to fill your income gap.

A better approach may be to systematically calculate how much of your retirement funds are needed to be placed into income-producing products. One of the products I often recommend, helping to fill the income gap with more certainty, is an *income annuity* issued by an insurance company. With an income annuity, there is no risk of taking out too much or too little each year, or of running out of money, as income annuities pay out for as long as you live. These payouts are based on the claims-paying ability of the insurer, so I only work with A-rated, top-tier insurance companies to accomplish this. In Chapter 10, I'll discuss the nuts and bolts of annuities in more detail.

Leaving your retirement income management to chance without a solid plan in place, and just taking your income out of cash or investments as needed, could create a retirement income crisis for yourself down the road. Longevity can result in undisciplined spending early in retirement, forcing you to dramatically cut back spending later in retirement. It can often have the opposite effect, instilling fear and frustration due to limited access to money, making it impossible to enjoy a stress-free retirement. Market risk can cause the same type of result if significant sums are liquidated while the market is down.

By contrast, if you can create reliable sources of retirement income with a portion of your investments and savings, you should be less exposed and able to ride out market volatility. This can allow your investments to do their job of helping protect you against the long-term negative effects of inflation. Once again, one of the most pragmatic ways to build security in retirement is to lock-down your *green "income" money* early with proper planning, so that these concerns are significantly minimized, if not completely eliminated.

Think of it this way: if you were nearing retirement and knew exactly how much money it would take to cover your expenses in retirement, why would you not carve out the money you need to fill the income gap today? Having a gap in retirement is like having a boat with holes in it – the bigger the gap (and the more holes in the boat), the faster the boat sinks. If you can seal the holes in the boat now before leaving the dock (creating sufficient positive cash flow throughout retirement), the boat should not sink, and the likelihood of a long and smooth journey is greatly enhanced. Because the future is so unpredictable, setting aside enough money to fill your retirement income gap helps you avoid the uncertainty of the market, and provides you with enough income so you won't run out of money in retirement.

To continue the boat analogy, if you are leaving the dock in a boat, it only makes sense to ensure the boat has everything it needs on board in case of disaster. If you send the boat out without any disaster preparations, and the boat springs an unexpected leak, you're out of luck. You either need to make it back to port, or the boat may sink. Don't take this approach with your retirement. If you have gaps in your retirement income plan, it's best to address this today. If you run out of money in retirement, please remember, there are no do-overs – the type of retirement you planned for yourself may be out of reach for good.

Instead of running this risk, consider carving out what you need to fill the gap now, and lock it down to reduce the chances that your retirement boat sinks at sea. Whatever is left over after that income gap is filled can be used for emergency or discretionary expenditures, and for longer-term growth, to combat inflation. Using this approach, certain funds are earmarked for income, and the remaining funds (red "risk" money) are allocated for the purpose of short-term and long-term growth. With this planning approach, your retirement income can be locked down regardless of what happens with your red money.

When working with clients to fill their retirement income gap, I back out a number from their savings and investments that takes into account inflation over their retirement lifetime, and I use that number as the starting point for calculating retirement income needs. If more money is needed down the road, it can be taken from the red "risk" money at that time. If inflation picks up, more funds can be peeled from long-term growth accounts to help maintain their standard of living in inflation-adjusted dollars. This is why it's not just a one-time adjustment, but an ongoing process that should be revisited annually between clients and advisors.

In the next two chapters, we'll take a deeper dive into green "income" money vs. red "risk" money.

CHAPTER 9

Your Green "Income" Money

"The man with a surplus controls circumstances, and the man without a surplus is controlled by circumstances."
– Henry Buckley

Earlier I spoke about how every dollar we have has a purpose, and understanding that purpose is critical to achieving a stress-free retirement. In order to do that, we must separate our money into two general categories: *green money* for lifetime income, and *red money* for long-term growth. In this chapter, I am going to discuss green "income" money in more detail.

Green "income" money can come in many different forms. For me to consider the money to be *green*, it has to meet certain criteria: it must be reliable, it must be lifetime, and it must be protected from outside forces – i.e. Social Security, pension, any other source of income that meets the criteria. If you find yourself without enough green income, there are things you can do to create more. Income-producing products can help fill the income gap, but need to be guaranteed, and by that, I mean it needs to produce reliable monthly cash flow, no matter what. One way to accomplish this is with income annuities, which can do something no other financial product can do – provide an additional monthly income stream for life. I devise a detailed income plan for my clients, so they know exactly how much money should be coming in each month in retirement – regardless of any "financial noise", or how any particular market performs. I will discuss annuities more in Chapter 11.

Retirement planning can often be a lot simpler than many financial advisors make it out to be. The main foundation of retirement planning lies in addressing the cash flow needs, or what I refer to as *core income*. This involves making sure you have enough income to cover your expenses throughout retirement, ensuring you maintain the same quality of life you enjoyed during your working years.

Having a proper income plan in place for life is like bulletproofing your retirement, insulating it from the volatility and fluctuations of the markets.

Planning for retirement without taking lifetime income into account is like building a house with a poor foundation – no matter how beautiful or well designed the house is, just a few cracks can weaken the entire structure; or worse, the whole house could collapse at any point. My job as a financial advisor is to help ensure my clients have enough core income when they retire, and that their cash flow foundation is strong and reliable. Our goal is to add these sources of income together to determine whether your projected retirement matches, exceeds, or falls short of your retirement income needs.

One of the biggest challenges I see facing retirees today is that the money coming from reliable sources in retirement is not sufficient enough to meet their expenses. To fill this gap, there are several choices available: cash-in your assets, take withdrawals from investments as needed, or convert some portion of them to income-producing assets. When sitting with our clients to help them find the right balance to fill this gap, we devise a viable strategy to generate enough core income to comfortably meet their retirement expenses. To accomplish this, we figure out the minimum amount of money you can take from other assets to fill the gap and address income needs, legacy planning, long-term care, and future investments. The remaining assets then become emergency money, and "fun money".

By projecting future expenses using reasonable assumptions about rates of return and inflation in retirement, we can identify potential gaps or surpluses with ease.

Income Planning

The green "income" money is unaffected by market pullbacks, corrections, or crashes. The monthly income continues like clockwork, regardless of outside influences. Stocks can go up, go down, or even move sideways for a long period of time, and it doesn't affect your fixed income one bit. In short, this is what I call, "smart retirement." This approach gives you the ability to invest your growth money without having to worry about whether you'll have enough monthly income in the event your return on red "risk" money doesn't meet your expectations.

Often, a financial advisor presents a retirement plan to a client by putting together a really nice presentation with charts and graphs, and by the time you're done reading it, if your eyes haven't already glazed over, you're actually more confused than when the meeting began. They'll put together a booklet that represents who you are and your goals, with some very attractive asset allocation models weaved into the fold. They often address income via withdrawal rates of 4% or even 5% a year from your investments. As long as you can beat that average in the market during retirement, you can't go wrong, right? What about the *what-ifs* in life when it comes to the market? What if the market goes through a 40% or 50% correction? What if we experience a flat, 10-year period with zero average market returns, like the S&P 500 performed between 1998-2008, dubbed "The Lost Decade"? Once again, a green "income" money approach can often take the guesswork out of retirement income planning and help ensure your income needs are met.

How to Calculate Your Monthly Income Needs

One of the first things to do when it comes to calculating your green "income" money is to perform a detailed budget analysis – what's coming in and what's going out. You should project 20, 30, and even 40 years into the future, and add inflation, all while making adjustments to the fixed expenses that fall off when appropriate – i.e. car loans, mortgages, etc. A great start is to detail your recurring monthly expenses. Here is a sample monthly expense and liabilities worksheet I use with my clients. It can be downloaded at:

http://www.plansmartretireright.com/worksheet

Monthly Expenses Worksheet

HOUSEHOLD

Mortgage – Principal / Interest	
Real Estate Taxes	
Homeowners Insurance	
Rent	
Renters Insurance	
Assoc Dues / Condo Fees	
Maintenance / Improvements	
House Cleaning	
Gas / Electricity	
Water / Sewer / Oil	
Cable / Internet / Cell Phones	
TOTALS	

TRANSPORTATION

Auto Loans / Leases	
Auto Insurance	
Repairs / Maintenance	
Commuting Costs - Gas / Tolls	
TOTALS	

DEBTS & OBLIGATIONS

Credit Cards / Loans	
Tuition / Student Loans	
Alimony	
Child Support	
TOTALS	

DAILY LIVING

Food - Groceries	
Food - Dining Out	
Clothing	
Personal Care	
TOTALS	

HEALTHCARE & INSURANCE

Health Insurance	
Prescriptions / Copays	
Dental	
Vision	
Life Insurance	
Long Term Care Insurance	
Disability Insurance	
Medicare	
Veterinarian	
TOTALS	

ENTERTAINMENT & RECREATION

Travel / Vacations	
Sports / Hobbies / Lessons	
Health Club	
Misc Entertainment	
TOTALS	

MISCELLANEOUS

Charitable Donations	
Gifts	
Subscriptions / Licenses / Dues	
Other	
TOTALS	

MONTHLY TOTAL

_____

After you have completed the expense worksheet, look at the numbers and determine if there is an *income gap* between what you have and what you need. Are you running a surplus or deficit after all expenses are paid? What will this expense worksheet look like in retirement if you want to maintain the same lifestyle? When there is a deficit, we often tend to pull money from our long-term growth funds to cover this amount. If the long-term growth funds are low or planned for something else, then we must cut expenses or work a little extra to cover this cash shortfall. If you're like the majority of my clients, I'll assume neither of those two are real options for you. Sure, we can work after retirement, but we'd like to do this only because we *want* to, not because we *have* to.

When it comes to examining and planning for the income gap, it's not how much money you make; it's how much money you keep, after all expenses and outflows. I meet with clients all the time that make a really good living, but when the majority of that money is going out for monthly expenses, they're not really saving - they're essentially living month-to-month. As you get closer to retirement, you may discover that your income won't be enough to meet your essential needs. If you find yourself in this situation, you'll have to adopt a plan to bridge this projected income gap. Ideally, as you can imagine, you'll be in a situation where you have positive monthly cash flow you can invest, enjoy or use for emergencies.

CHAPTER 10

Your Red "Risk" Money

Now that you have a deeper understanding of how to secure a stress-free retirement by addressing your green "income" money, this chapter is going to explore the red "risk" money in detail. Red "risk" money can fluctuate over time and is earmarked for short-term and long-term growth. It can be invested in different levels of risk with the objective of a reasonable rate of return over time – not too much risk, or too little – a good balance, based on your time horizon, objectives and risk tolerance. Usually, the higher the expected returns, the higher the risk to achieve those returns. Too much risk can result in the potential for big losses, while too little risk may subject your money to the danger of not keeping up with inflation. I will touch more on this in chapter 12. Either way, it's important to understand that the terms "at risk" and "risky" are very different things.

When focusing on red "risk" money, I believe it should meet certain criteria: be globally diversified, actively managed (staying flexible whereas the investments are constantly adjusted or tweaked to meet your goals, objectives, and risk tolerance), and a portion of the funds should be invested into assets that are protected from negative trends in the market.

The key to the successful utilization of your red "risk" money is to first understand asset allocation and diversification, which are still the foundation for growing your assets while controlling portfolio risk. Making tactical changes to your asset mix, while maintaining a longer-term perspective, allows you to respond to market opportunities in an attempt to minimize risk.

Asset Allocation & Diversification

We've all heard the phrase, *"Don't put all your eggs in one basket."* Fun fact: while this expression was first linked to Miguel Cervantes, who wrote *Don Quixote* in 1605, it has not changed its core meaning over the years – it still means not putting all of your resources into any one endeavor. This concept remains as important as ever in investment risk mitigation. Many interpret this in different ways, but when it comes_to managing your investments and savings in retirement, it's important to understand that asset allocation and diversification can be your best ally in surviving financial volatility and achieving a stress-free retirement.

Sure, turbulence happens and things get choppy, but a properly allocated and diversified portfolio mix should help you steer clear of huge downswings and market chaos. Proper allocation and diversification can likely be the biggest determinant of your investment returns over time. Deciding on the correct balance of investments is one of the most critical decisions investors make. Don't take it lightly.

In its simplest form, *asset allocation* is the percentage of your portfolio invested in stocks, bonds, and cash. Your asset allocation is the primary determinant of the risk level within your investment portfolio. While stocks are often considered the most aggressive investments in a typical asset allocation model, bonds are a middle-of-the-road option, while cash and other cash alternatives like savings accounts, money markets and CD's, are often the safest way to invest your money.

Diversification is simply a risk management technique that involves spreading your money amongst many different asset classes, and investing into a wide variety of financial products within those asset classes, thus preventing your entire portfolio from suffering losses all at once. The higher the risk of your portfolio, the higher the return you should expect over time. This is known as the risk/reward relationship and has to do with the theory of how risk increases – there is typically an increase in potential reward in order for the investment to be perceived as being "worth the risk", or a fair tradeoff for that risk.

As stated earlier, there is no one-size-fits-all way to do this, and the overarching theme is that you should avoid putting all of your money into one specific asset class or sector. Instead, allocate these funds to a broad spectrum of asset classes – the broader the better. Sure, if you correctly choose the best performing stock or asset class, the returns can prove to be extremely lucrative; however, the risk is also just as great. The best approach to asset allocation and diversification is one that is customized, disciplined, and tailored to your individual needs.

Global Diversification

"Don't look for the needle in the haystack. Just buy the haystack." – John Bogle

---

In my opinion, red "risk" money should be diversified across a large variety of asset classes within many different markets and countries around the world. This can be accomplished by building a globally diversified portfolio through strategic asset allocation and proper diversification of your savings in the widest array of investment options. A globally diversified portfolio takes this one step further and spreads your money across as many global, non-correlated asset classes as possible. This can ensure your money is not subject to the same volatility as a portfolio that solely relies on U.S. equities or U.S. bonds. Here is a diagram of what we consider to be a global investment portfolio. Before you try to determine what percentage of your money should go where, it's important to understand your goals, objectives and risk tolerance.

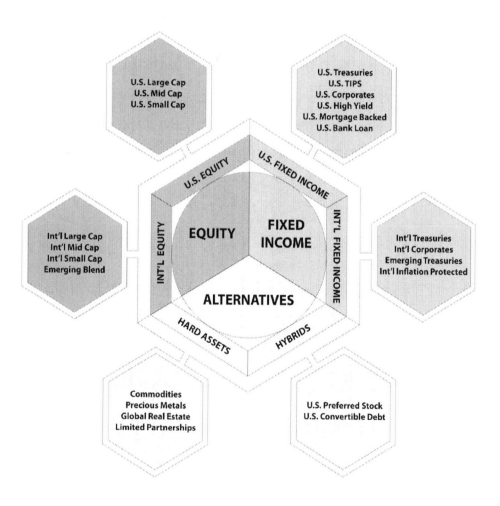

When the market experiences severe pullbacks, and other portfolios may be subject to bigger losses, a globally diversified portfolio, spread out over a number of different markets, can typically suffer less. This type of portfolio is not dependent upon one specific sector or asset class. The diversified plans I put together for my clients give them extreme confidence that not only should they be able to weather market storms, but they can actually come out ahead when all is said and done.

Outside this investment portfolio mix, there are other assets, like annuities, which can position some money with the potential to earn interest when the market is up, and de-risk with principal protection when the market is down. Adding annuities to a portfolio can help smooth out the long-term return pattern of a portfolio. It's sort of like playing offense and defense at the same time. Later, I will discuss the different types of annuities one may wish to add to their retirement strategy.

Perhaps retooling your investment portfolio and taking advantage of all the available instruments in the marketplace can help you enjoy a more financially secure and comfortable retirement. Gone are the days when a portfolio of U.S. stocks and bonds, some international market exposure, and some alternative investments were enough to be considered "diversified." Now, we can take diversification to the next level by combining a broad overlay across a variety of global asset classes with a non-traditional approach that offers a much deeper level of diversification.

Safety Through Diversification

When we talk about the word "safe", what does that mean to you? Most people will say it stands for protection: no risk, no loss, no downside. Who can say that in 2008, or during any major market correction, that they were invested in one stock, or one bond? The truth is, everyone was likely more or less diversified, right? So, if your investments were spread out over many funds, stocks, ETFs, etc., did you lose any money in 2008?

The answer is likely "yes". So, when we hear that we are "safer" by diversifying, what does that really mean? Perhaps what we feel is fully diversified, isn't *really* diversified. Over time, it's been proven that a well-diversified portfolio can *reduce* risk, but not *eliminate* it. While I believe it is necessary to take some risk with the goals of growing our money and offsetting the long-term effects of inflation, I also believe you need to analyze your individual situation - your goals, your income, and your assets - and plan carefully, so you know what "safe" looks like for your retirement dollars.

Over Time, the Market Outperforms Everything

I hear this phrase often when in client meetings, and I like to put it into perspective. While it may be true that over the long haul a properly diversified and allocated portfolio may outperform many other types of investments, this belief needs to be reevaluated, or scaled back, in retirement. Sure, over time the markets are efficient, profitable, and one of the biggest reasons we're able to grow and live off our retirement nest egg. However, as we get older, this rule becomes less applicable, and our mindset must change. In retirement, it's not about the biggest possible return anymore; it's about a shift towards a reasonable rate on our money, with principal protection as a core way of thinking.

In my opinion, portfolios should include many asset classes, each with different risk characteristics and rates of return. More specifically, I often advise clients to move investment assets into index funds, due to their broad diversification and tax efficiency. *Index funds* are a type of mutual fund with a portfolio constructed to match or track the components of a market index, such as the *Standard & Poor's 500 Index* (S&P 500). Index funds have proven over time to outperform many active managers, and index funds typically carry lower investment fees compared to those of the average mutual fund. During an extended period of time, these reduced costs can often add to your overall investment returns.

The end goal is to have a carefully balanced approach based on your individual risk profile. This theory has proven successful over time because different asset classes don't always move in tandem, and their movements are unpredictable. Therefore, their short-term returns, for the most part, are completely random. Over time, the strategy of being in every asset class vs. a select few should not only provide you with more consistent long-term growth on your investments, but also serve as a hedge against huge crashes or corrections in any one market, helping to provide a cushion in case things go wrong. The majority of my clients know asset allocation and diversification are core components of their long-term financial success. I enjoy educating clients on our investment process, and the logic involved in such an approach. This gives them the peace of mind that comes with knowing why they own what they own, and the reasoning behind each financial decision that is made.

There are no cookie-cutter methods to tackling asset allocation and diversification. It first has to be determined what you are trying to achieve – a need or a goal. It's really all about financial priorities and identifying what gaps you may have in your financial plan. It's about where you are, and where you want or need to be. If your goal is, "I want to retire with $1,000,000 in 10 years", or, "I want to relocate to a warmer climate in 5 years," these are both examples of what I like to refer to as *goal-based planning*. On the flip side, there is a school of thought where it makes no sense to aim for a financial goal, when the more urgent concern is about whether or not current or future expenses can be met. An example of this is, "I want to ensure I have enough money to last beyond my life expectancy", or, "I want to make sure I can live the same lifestyle in retirement I had while working." I refer to this as *needs-based planning*. Can you run calculations and answer questions like these on your own? It may be a challenge without proper planning software. And we're talking about the financial health of your retirement. The stakes are high!

When working with clients, I help them complete an assessment which identifies their objectives, risk tolerance, and time horizon. This helps me build a customized portfolio for them – one that is as individual and unique as they are. Of course, there is no single approach that's right for everyone, but I am a strong believer that working with a financial advisor is a great start to constructing your diversified investment plan.

CHAPTER 11

Annuities in a Retirement Plan

I am a firm believer that annuities as a whole can do things no other financial product can do. They bring certainties to an uncertain financial plan and investment portfolio. However, choosing the wrong annuity can turn out to be a huge mistake. If you are interested in purchasing an annuity, I highly recommended you look for a competent financial advisor that specializes in annuities. These products have a lot of moving parts and with the myriad of options available, can be complex. The right advisor should be able to help you navigate the waters and select the correct annuity for your particular situation with ease. If you don't fully understand the product, or you feel it hasn't been properly explained to you, my advice would be to hold off. Don't buy it.

Due to misconceptions and misinformation surrounding annuities, I will explain, in general terms, the four popular types of annuities available today. There are many annuity products in the marketplace with a wide variety of riders, add-ons, investment strategies, fees, and tax considerations. If you want an in-depth explanation of the ins-and-outs of a specific annuity type, you should discuss it with a financial advisor or insurance agent with specific expertise in the field.

One general note when it comes to annuities: age matters. Annuities are retirement products whereas similar to early withdrawals from an IRA, once you put money in, you may face early withdrawal penalties should you need to access the funds prior to your retirement age. There are a few exceptions to this rule, but typically, it's a bad idea to touch these funds until you reach age 59 ½.

Deferred Annuities vs. Immediate Annuities

As a whole, annuities fall into one of two categories: *deferred annuities* or *immediate annuities*. The terms deferred annuity and immediate annuity simply indicate when the distribution (income) phase of the annuity begins. This refers to when you plan on taking money out. Both types of annuities can provide, upon election, a continuous stream of payments for life.

With a *deferred annuity*, you make a lump sum, or a series of premium payments, and your money has the potential to earn interest during what is referred to as the *accumulation phase*. With this type of annuity, you benefit from the power of tax deferral, and the interest wouldn't be taxed until it's withdrawn.

Immediate annuities allow you to convert a lump sum of cash into an immediate lifetime income stream. They differ from deferred annuities in that they have no accumulation period. They are funded with a single lump-sum payment, rather than through a series of premium payments. The income payments start no later than one year after the premium has been received by the insurance company.

Now that we've briefly touched on the two main categories of deferred and immediate annuities, let's look at some of the most common types of annuities in the marketplace.

The 4 Most Common Types of Annuities

Fixed Annuity

Fixed annuities are tax deferred savings vehicles that pay investors a fixed interest rate for a specified period of time. They are similar to bank CD's, but guaranteed by insurance companies rather than by the FDIC. Like CD's, fixed annuities pay guaranteed rates of interest, in many cases higher than bank CD's. They can offer attractive interest rates for both short-term or long-term accumulation, and these terms typically range from 3 years to 10 years. However, if your liquidity needs are more time-sensitive, short-term CD's may serve you better.

Earnings on CD's are taxable in the year the interest is earned, and even if you don't take the money out, you receive a 1099 for the interest accrued throughout the year. With fixed annuities, earnings accumulate tax deferred, and are not treated as taxable income until they are withdrawn. If you don't need the money when the annuity expires, you can often roll the money into another annuity. For investors who want to beat CD rates but don't want to invest in a market-linked vehicle, this can be a place to park funds in a low-risk, tax-deferred investment.

Fixed Indexed Annuity (FIA)

Fixed indexed annuities (sometime referred to as equity indexed annuities) are tax deferred growth products which accumulate interest based on the performance of a stock market index (i.e. NASDAQ, S&P 500) rather than a specific interest rate. FIA's enable you to participate in a market index, and earn interest when the market goes up, while offering principal protection if the market goes down. The index annuity's growth is subject to rate floors and caps, meaning it cannot exceed or fall below the specified return levels, even if the underlying index fluctuates outside of those set parameters.

You benefit from guaranteed principal while participating in market gains, without being vulnerable to market declines.

Essentially, if the market goes up, you get credited some interest based on your investment strategy. However, when the market goes down, regardless of how much, your principal is protected and your account value stays where it is, minus any rider fees and costs, if applicable. There are other optional riders (add-ons) that can be purchased with FIA's based on your future needs and goals, so it's a good idea to explore these as well. For example, one of the most popular riders offered is what's referred to as an *income rider*, which allows you to create a lifetime income stream when needed most.

There are many products of this type available that can be issued by a number of insurance companies, so make sure you understand all the nuances before investing. FIA's are an excellent asset class to consider as part of an overall diversified portfolio, and they can be a great alternative or complement to a bond portfolio. These products can be difficult to understand, so I recommend you speak to an insurance agent or financial advisor that specializes in FIA's to make sure you get the annuity that's right for your particular situation.

Variable Annuity (VA)

Variable annuities are tax deferred investment vehicles which allow buyers to make an investment with the insurer and allocate their money according to a menu of mutual funds (sub-accounts) allowed by the contract. The returns from a VA vary within the sub-accounts, and these contract values fluctuate based on the ups and downs of the market. Typically, there is no limit on the amount of money you can invest in such annuities, so they offer an opportunity to set aside additional tax-deferred money for retirement, if you've already reached the limit of tax-deductible funds you can place in a retirement plan, such as a 401(k) or SEP-IRA.

These types of annuities typically come with high annual fees, which should be fully understood before making a purchase. VA fee structures are often complex, and can be associated with management fees, annual fees, administrative fees, charges for special add-on benefits, annual mortality fees, and expense-risk charges. The underlying mutual funds in a VA also generally carry internal fees. It's probably a good idea to read the prospectus that accompany these products, so you understand the investment choices and fees, and have a solid grasp of exactly how the annuity works. Like FIA's, VA's also come with the ability to add additional options and guarantees via riders, based on your long-term objectives.

Single Premium Immediate Annuity (SPIA)

Single premium immediate annuities (or income annuities) are contracts with an insurance company which allow you to give the company a lump sum of money in exchange for a guaranteed monthly, yearly, or a lifelong income stream, depending on the payout option you select. One of the biggest challenges many face in retirement is not having enough predictable monthly income to cover expenses or meet desired cash flow, which we previously discussed as *core income*. When retirement income doesn't meet monthly expenses, we typically proceed to draw down other assets that are intended for long-term growth. SPIA's give the contract owner the ability to turn on a lifetime income stream and "pensionize" it to help cover any potential income gaps as they retire. In my opinion, income annuities are great assets, and one of the best ways to address longevity risk. As a reminder, many annuities (as mentioned above) give the annuity holder the ability to add a lifetime income rider if they desire. This is similar to that of a SPIA.

By adding SPIA's to an income plan, retirees can ensure they cover at least their basic living expenses (not covered by pensions, Social Security, or other reliable income streams). With SPIA's in a diversified portfolio, you have greater flexibility in other areas of your retirement plan, including the ability to take more investment risk with the remaining portfolio. Income annuities, when added to a wide mix of stocks and bonds, have been academically proven over the years to extend retirement portfolios. In 2007, a study co-sponsored by New York Life Insurance and the Wharton Financial Institution Center at the University of Pennsylvania ("*Investing Your Lump Sum at Retirement*"), identified lifetime income annuities as the most cost-effective and least risky asset class for generating guaranteed retirement income for life.

This study also revealed that income annuities can provide secure income for one's entire lifetime for 25-40% less money than it would cost an individual to provide a similar level of secure lifetime income through traditional means. Further, the study highlighted that consumers are not annuitizing enough of their portfolios, even though income annuities are low-cost, available from creditworthy insurers, and provide guaranteed payments for life. Equities, fixed income, and other investment products like mutual funds carry the risk of outliving one's nest egg.

Weighing Your Options

When it comes to annuities, you have the flexibility to tailor a plan that meets your individual needs. Ultimately, the appropriateness of annuities is dependent upon your circumstances, financial goals, time horizon, tax situation, and the purpose of the money you are considering placing into an annuity. Know what you want, become educated on the details, and then balance the logical sides of the decision. With a variety of optional payout methods, you have the flexibility to choose a plan that fits your retirement needs.

When it comes to deciding where to park your hard-earned dollars, I highly recommend consulting with a qualified financial advisor or insurance agent with deep knowledge of the annuity marketplace to help you weigh the advantages and disadvantages of annuities for your individual retirement plan. Annuities aren't a solution for everyone, and you shouldn't buy one unless it's appropriate for your specific situation.

CHAPTER 12

Retirement Investing Pitfalls

Experience has taught us that successful investing requires discipline and patience. A long-term investment focus can help when emotions run high. While balancing ongoing changes in the economy and market can seem challenging, a steady course can help buffer you against turbulence and uncertainty. While I believe there isn't one right approach to investing for your retirement, there are, in fact, a number of commonly encountered pitfalls many investors make. How can you avoid making mistakes which have the potential to devastate your retirement? Knowledge. When it comes to retirement planning, knowledge is the best defense. The more you know about the pitfalls that can derail your retirement, the better prepared you should be when it comes to avoiding them.

In previous chapters, I've discussed risk management and asset allocation as important components of the retirement planning process. In this chapter, I want to dive into some of the specific situations that can pose dangers to your retirement.

"*Forewarned is forearmed*", as the saying goes – knowing what to look out for can help you steer clear of investing decisions which can imperil your retirement plan, and ultimately, your life savings.

Trying to Time the Market

When markets rally or pull back, attempting to find the top to sell or the bottom to buy may seem tempting. The problem, however, is that investors usually guess wrong, potentially missing out on the best market plays. One reason is attempting to time the market and predict future market movements. This sounds great in theory, but market timing works about as well as fortune telling. Essentially, by trying to time the market, you are relying on speculation instead of certainties. When people invest on the high and pull out on the low, they may miss opportunities by not remaining patient. The problem is that equity gains can often be made in a very short amount of time. If you are not in the market when it moves, you may miss out on the whole play.

The bottom line - accurately chasing the market's top and bottom is virtually impossible. A better approach may be to make small adjustments that can help you stay the course. As my experience has proven, time *in* the market matters more than the timing *of* the market.

Taking Too Much Risk

Not accurately timing the markets is one thing. Another common mistake is having too much risk in your portfolio. Risk involves the chance that the investments you choose can lose or perform differently than you anticipate.

During the bull market days of the mid 1990s and early 2000s, money poured into equities – often into risky tech and internet stocks. The value stocks trading low had many of their investors wanting to chase higher returns. When a bear market followed the tragic events of 9/11, the bottom fell out of the tech sector; meanwhile, many value stocks weathered the storm. Investors who took on too much risk – not wanting to miss out on the dot-com boom – most likely saw their portfolios take a severe beating.

Portfolio risk can be deceptive. Holding a diverse mix of stocks, bonds, and alternatives may seem adequate for managing risk, but it's just one component. If you own correlated investments – meaning they move in similar patterns – then you could be jeopardizing your portfolio. If the investments respond to market declines all in the same way, you may increase the risk of losing all your money. The objective is to take on the amount of risk that is aligned with your long-term goals.

Taking Too Little Risk

As we now see, taking too much risk in retirement can be dangerous. Playing the market cautiously and taking on too little risk may also negatively affect your portfolio. While minimal risk can feel like a safe move, you could miss important market rallies. During periods of market turbulence, many investors tend to flock to low-risk investments like U.S. Treasuries and cash. This aversion to risk can affect long-term investments, as too many fixed-rate investments can put a cap on your portfolio's profitability.

By trying to reduce portfolio losses, however, investors may be trading one type of risk for others: inflation, high valuations, and greater-than-expected volatility. While equities can typically have greater loss potential than short-term, fixed-rate investments, they also can have a greater potential for gain. For many investors, hunkering down only in safe haven investments may hinder the growth of an investment portfolio. Inflation is a serious concern in long-term investing, and too little growth in your investments can leave you with a shortfall in your retirement years. With inflation eating away at cash every year, most investors need at least some growth-oriented investments.

Underestimating Market Risk (Not Properly Diversifying)

While the stock market has historically offered better performance than other asset classes, such as government and corporate bonds, this type of performance comes with a drawback: higher risk. And of course, this makes sense when the following investment principle is considered: along with the potential for higher returns, comes higher risk.

I've met with many investors over the years who are overly aggressive and have placed a substantial portion of their retirement savings in stock market-related investments, even when such an allocation may involve taking on more risk than is prudent, given their investment time horizon, age, and risk tolerance. They run the risk of a market crash adversely affecting their retirement income because there isn't enough time for their retirement investments to replenish funds lost in a crash prior to entering retirement.

While there are many variables to consider when addressing risk (time horizons, risk tolerance, goals, other assets), you really want to achieve an appropriate balance of risk in your investments, as discussed in Chapter 10. Taking too little risk can yield too little return and can ultimately cost you over the long haul. This is why it's crucial when planning for retirement to understand that simply diversifying among different stocks or ETFs may not be sufficient, especially if all of these investments are part of the same market, sector or class. The strategy of investing in a large variety of non-correlated assets (assets that make money independently but don't necessarily correlate with one another) spread across many asset classes should be utilized.

Another important aspect of becoming fully diversified is to invest in global markets. This enables you to reduce the risk of the U.S. market underperforming overseas markets, and thus hurting your overall returns. Global diversification has also been proven to lessen a portfolio's volatility, as it won't be as sensitive to returns from any single market.

Recency Bias

This is the tendency of people to purchase investments which have recently performed well. This type of behavior typically manifests in people chasing the top performing stocks, mutual funds, or ETFs in a particular year with the belief that this performance is likely to be repeated going forward. However, often the opposite may happen, and the top performing investments in any one year or years may turn out to be poor performers in the following years.

As a financial advisor, a big part of my job is explaining effects such as this to investors who are tempted to invest their hard-earned savings based on recent performance, rather than taking long-term considerations into account. Investors who chase the latest hot-performing investments run the risk of hurting the long-term performance of their retirement savings. Investments that outperform over a certain period of time can often underperform over the period of time that directly follows. In most cases, the saying holds true: *"what goes up, must come down."*

To avoid falling victim to recency bias, it's important to view the performance of asset classes over an extended time period, perhaps a 10-year time frame, at a minimum. This means you need to be able to stick to your long-term strategy, be patient, and ride out the ups and downs. Investing a disproportionate amount in one sector on the basis of recent outperformance subjects your portfolio to the risk of underperforming in the next period. Broadly diversifying your portfolio reduces the risk of this type of subpar performance, and offers a more measured approach to achieving your retirement savings objectives.

The Clustering Illusion (The Hot Hand Fallacy)

The clustering illusion is the belief that things that happen in bunches or clusters are not random events, but instead constitute meaningful phenomena. For instance, while many studies have shown that active mutual fund managers, on average, underperform broad indices such as the S&P 500, investors often invest in fund managers who've beaten the S&P

500 for the past few years on the assumption that they may continue to do so.

While there are certainly fund managers that have the skill to consistently outperform the market, in many cases a fund manager's success can be attributed to other factors, such as breaking news or market conditions, rather than the manager's skill set. Subsequently, as these market conditions change, many of these managers wind up underperforming, which contributes to the high turnover at many of these firms and can be a frustrating experience for investors. Given the difficulty in determining whether a particular investment manager has enough skill (or luck) to provide performance that make up for the fees involved in paying for the manager's services, to most of my clients, the use of low-cost ETFs is instead more appealing.

The natural tendency to buy funds run by managers with good recent track records, even those no more likely to outperform than other managers, is also known as the "hot hand fallacy." To illustrate how the phenomenon works, let's use a basketball analogy. When players pass the ball to a player who has made a number of shots in a row recently, on the assumption that player is more likely to make the next shot, the hot hand fallacy is at play. The fact is, the player being passed the ball more often is no more likely to make the next shot after making a series of shots than their typical shooting percentage would suggest.

Prospect Theory

Prospect theory centers on this illogical financial behavior: if two equal choices are put before an individual, with one presented in terms of potential gains and the other in terms of possible losses, investors are typically more focused on avoiding losses. This results in *loss aversion*, which makes investors reluctant to sell an investment they have a loss in, until it returns to breakeven or better, even though this can be a suboptimal approach to managing their investments.

According to prospect theory, losses have more emotional impact than an equivalent amount of gains. For example, in a traditional way of thinking, the perceived benefit gained from receiving $50 should be equal to a situation in which you gained $100, and then lost $50. In both situations, the end result is a net gain of $50. However, despite the fact that you still end up with a $50 gain in either case, most people view a single gain of $50 more favorably than gaining $100 and then losing $50.

Another investor tendency explored by prospect theory is the *sunk cost* fallacy. This refers to an investment approach that results in investors continuing to invest in a losing investment, in effect throwing good money after bad, even in the face of negative company or sector developments. Based on this theory, an investor would be better served "throwing in the towel" and walking away, instead of letting their emotions get the best of them, while continuing to follow a down trend with the hopes of it turning around. Prospect theory and the sunk cost fallacy can adversely affect your investment returns if you are not careful.

Individual Stock Investments
(Excessive Single-Stock Risk)

Each investor should decide how he or she wants to approach retirement investing. This is true whether you choose to pick investments yourself or hire an advisor to do it for you. In either case, if the approach you follow involves investing in individual stocks, you should be aware of the risks involved.

Please note this is not to say that I believe investors should never buy individual stocks. While the approach I favor focuses on ETFs as a way to benefit from the growth potential of stocks while taking advantage of the diversification of an index, this doesn't mean that individual stock investing can't be a viable option. However, such an approach can expose you to certain risks, foremost of which is a lack of diversification.

Taking excessive company or single stock risk is another way of saying that an investor's portfolio is not sufficiently diversified. As covered earlier, market risk is the risk that the stock market falls as a whole, where company risk is the risk that something occurs relative to an individual company, causing the company's stock to decline. This type of risk can be dangerous for your retirement investments in an undiversified portfolio, potentially exposing your assets to the risks of just one or two negative events across a spectrum of market sector or company disruptions.

For instance, if your portfolio consists of a couple of stocks and one of them enters bankruptcy, losing 100 percent of its value, your overall portfolio is likely to be significantly impaired, even if the market has been performing well. In an ETF tracking the S&P 500 index, on the other hand, a catastrophic event affecting one or more of the companies within the index won't have the same devastating effect on the value of your investment, given that each company only makes up a small part of the overall value of the index. Thus, while ETFs are subject to market risk, which can generally be addressed by diversifying among a variety of non-correlated asset classes, they largely eliminate the company risk associated with owning only a few individual stocks.

Why do investors fall into the trap of taking excessive company risk with their retirement money? There are several reasons for excessive risk-taking of this type. One of the most prominent of which is the *unbalanced loss effect.*

The Unbalanced Loss Effect

Let's say you buy a stock for $100 a share, and the stock declines in value to $70 per share. You have suffered a 30%

loss in the value of the stock. Now ask yourself, how much would the stock have to rise in value for you to get back to breakeven? 30% might seem like the obvious answer, but it is in fact incorrect. 30% of $70 is $21, meaning that if the stock rises 30% after falling 30%, its value will be $91; $9 short of the breakeven point of $100. In fact, the stock must actually rise approximately 43% to get back to $100 ($70 x 43% = $30).

This is known as the *unbalanced loss effect*. Investors who don't understand this effect may be prone to taking larger risks, with bigger portions of their retirement investments, than is prudent, simply because they don't realize the devastating impact steep losses on investments can have on their portfolio's performance.

The Herding Effect

While the herding affect in animals is well documented, its impact on investors has come into focus in recent years as well. We are a social species, so it's no surprise people find comfort in doing things together. This tendency is easy to see in a wide variety of social circumstances such as sporting events, cultural events, and even fads that sweep across a population, only to fade away almost as fast as they began (fidget spinners, Pokémon, roller discos, mullets, etc.)

When it comes to investing, investors are more likely to invest in a stock if it seems to be popular with other investors, friends or family members, perhaps due to this same herding instinct. While this may be helpful (or at least harmless) in social situations, when dealing with investing, it can be counterproductive. Given that a fundamental investing principle is to buy low and sell high, if a stock is already popular among investors, the price may be at an elevated level. So, investors buying into the stock at these higher prices may be taking more risk than is prudent, especially when investing for retirement.

Not Taking Advantage of Professional Investment Advice

Being unaware of these pitfalls can potentially lead you down a path to an unfavorable and undesirable investment outcome. Having professional guidance to help you make sound, logical investment decisions should help you overcome your own irrational perspectives. A long-term investment outlook requires a personalized strategy that accounts for your current and future needs, time horizon, and appetite for risk.

Successful long-term investing requires the ability to position and rebalance your portfolio to ride bear and bull markets. This level of complexity can make working with an investment professional critical to meeting your goals. Chasing returns and following cookie-cutter approaches on your own is risky. I believe successfully navigating the turbulent investing world of today requires training, prudent management, and committing to a long-term, active investing strategy.

CHAPTER 13

Employer Retirement Plans

People spend decades working in their careers and saving up money for retirement in their company-sponsored retirement plan. Despite their best intentions to ensure they've invested their retirement savings the most optimal way possible, many people don't have much understanding of how to manage these retirement accounts after they retire. Handling these accounts correctly in retirement is just as important as managing growth during their working years.

When it comes to retirement, many important decisions have to be made to align your financial "ducks in a row". One of the most important decisions is to figure out what to do with the company retirement plan you've built up working over the years. Whether the plan is a 401(k), 403(b), TSP, or 457, you certainly need to evaluate your options and understand them well. As the old saying goes, *what you don't know might hurt you.*

Since there are certain nuances and rules that apply to each employer plan, you can speak with the plan administrator or your human resources department to determine which options are available to you. In this section, I will briefly cover the most basic retirement plan options you'll have when you retire, so you're more prepared to make the choice that benefits you and your family the most.

1. Leave the account in your old employer's retirement plan

Many retirement plan administrators charge record-keeping and other fees to manage your account, regardless of whether you are still employed with the company. These fees can take a significant bite out of your future net worth, especially if you have accounts maintained at several different employers. While this may be the most convenient option available, please keep in mind there may be some disadvantages to consider.

For starters, your current employer retains control over your investment options, and you are often limited to the investment choices and withdrawal flexibility they offer. With these limited options, you may not have access to the investment vehicles that could be more appropriate for you, or better suited to help you achieve your desired retirement goals. Further, keep in mind that by leaving your money in your old employer's plan, you are required to manage these assets throughout retirement. Unfortunately, most people don't have the time or knowledge to do this.

Another item worth thinking about is the limited access to professional investment advice. By rolling over your account into an individual retirement account (IRA), you are essentially moving it through a nontaxable transfer to another financial institution or custodian, where it continues to grow tax-deferred. With a rollover, you have the ability to work with a licensed advisor and are typically provided more flexibility and greater investment options. I will discuss this further in a bit.

The bottom line is, if your company plan is terrific, with lots of investment options and low fees, keeping your funds there may make sense. However, I feel there are significant benefits to moving an employer-sponsored plan to an IRA you control, so you should carefully consider which approach makes the most sense for you given your financial goals.

2. Rollover the account to the new employer's retirement plan

Practically speaking, this option is usually available if the employee leaves their current employer and begins employment with another company. In many cases, the new employer can allow the retirement funds to rollover into the new company plan. It may turn out to be the best option, as it is simplest to do. But how do you know if it's the *right* choice for you? The decision should be heavily weighed by the investment options and fees of the new retirement plan versus the old plan. As far as disadvantages, you may run into the same issues as discussed with the previous option. Furthermore, you may also be putting all of your eggs into one basket with the investments offered by your new employer.

By keeping some of your retirement assets separate (not all rolled into one account), you can take advantage of different investment approaches and the benefits of spreading your assets out even more through diversification. The good news is that if you're unsatisfied with the choices available to you, rolling your money into an IRA may be a better option, and would provide you greater control of your investments.

3. *Rollover the account to an IRA*

For most people, completing a rollover to an individual retirement account (IRA) is almost always the preferable choice when pulling money out of an employer's retirement plan. This is because rolling over your company plan to an IRA with a financial institution allows your retirement money to continue to grow tax-deferred while providing maximum control of the retirement assets and more investment options.

Since rolling your account over into an IRA typically provides access to professional investment advice, you often

156

find that this advice is more personalized and can offer fully customizable asset allocation models to help you meet your retirement goals. Ultimately, this option usually provides you the most amount of flexibility, control, and investment options. A financial professional can assist with rollovers, if this is something you wish to do.

Note: You'd definitely want to make sure to have the money directly transferred from the company plan to a financial institution, or you run the risk of incurring taxes and penalties.

4. Take the lump sum as a distribution and cash out the proceeds

This certainly should be a last resort. Cashing out a company retirement account, in my opinion, is the single worst investment decision an individual can make with regards to their company retirement plan. This move could trigger significant tax consequences and penalties. Sure, there may be a really good reason for doing this due to a serious financial crunch, but I'd certainly recommend holding off at all costs. You see, the tragedy is far greater than the taxes and penalty alone; the greater financial loss comes from the decades of tax-deferred compounding that money could have earned, had the account owner chosen to initiate a retirement plan rollover instead. Before considering a lump sum distribution, I recommend sitting down with a tax advisor to discuss the potential tax consequences.

5. Annuitize your retirement account into a lifetime income annuity with monthly payments

While this option isn't available with all employer-sponsored retirement plans, this is certainly something to consider if it is. "Annuitization" is when you trade in your retirement account for lifetime income payments, and "pensionize" these retirement funds. You are basically purchasing an annuity from an insurance company that pays a monthly benefit to you for life. The annuity would be purchased for you from the company's annuity provider. In its basic form, with a life annuity, you can choose either a *single life annuity*, an annuity that provides monthly payments to you only as long as you live, or a *joint life annuity*, an annuity that provides monthly payments to you while you and the person with whom you choose to share your annuity (your "joint annuitant") are alive.

Quite often, these products can be attractive options for someone with monthly cash flow issues, but there are some things that need to be considered. The first and most obvious is that you lose access to your principal. If you choose the lifetime income option, you no longer have access to this money, as it has been converted to a lifetime monthly income stream. Also, if you choose the income option on your life only and something happens to you early in retirement, there would be no death benefit for your spouse or loved ones. When you start withdrawals from a retirement plan, taxes could be due whether you take a lump sum distribution, partial distribution, or withdraw via annuitization; so, planning ahead is needed to account for this.

Obviously, many variables exist when it comes to retirement planning, but obtaining the necessary information ahead of time, and having a sound and disciplined approach as you head into retirement, can make all the difference. Before you choose which option is best for you, I recommend you analyze the pros and cons of each with your financial advisor to see which works best for your particular situation. These choices can be a bit overwhelming, but I'm confident you and your loved ones can benefit from thinking them through.

CHAPTER 14

A Comprehensive Retirement Analysis – Bringing it All Together

Are You Retirement Ready?

Whether you're planning for retirement or you're already there, these are some questions to keep in mind when determining if you're retirement ready. Retirement readiness is not just feeling ready to retire, but being able to get through retirement, regardless of how long it may last. Are you ready to make it through retirement? Are you retirement ready in the sense of having accumulated the necessary assets? If you stop working, do you have enough saved? The sooner you address these questions, the more time you'll have to make the necessary adjustments to put yourself on the path of a stress-free retirement.

Determining your retirement readiness.

The decisions you make regarding work, income, expenses, etc. can all play a part in what your retirement could look like. Of course, with every decision, there are tradeoffs and consequences. In my opinion, the following questions are key to consider when determining if you are retirement ready.

When do you want to retire?

This is the first thing you need to know. You really start looking at retirement differently when there is an end date in mind. If you think about your life, from the day you start kindergarten to the day you start college, everything is mapped out for you. Each step you need to take along the way to get to the next level is specified in advance.

The challenge with retirement is we don't treat it this way. People often go into it willy-nilly, without a clear plan. Also, the majority of people I meet would retire as soon as possible if they knew they could afford it. Why not have a plan for retirement like schooling, one you can follow step by step? Just as it helps us to be structured when attending school and pursuing educational goals, retirement should be no different. This is why you should at least have a date set for retirement.

Without knowing when you plan to retire, determining how long your money can last is extremely difficult.

Deciding when you plan to retire is the hardest question to answer because it relies on much more than simply calculating how long a certain amount of money could last. The answer to this question also relies upon projections for what you need and want, and what will make you happy in the future. Still, this is a question that must be answered. How can you plan for retirement if you don't know the date you *want* to retire or the date you *can* retire? This date is the most important variable of all when it comes to retirement planning. Once we have this pinned down, we can evaluate the priorities, decide what adjustments should be made, and put an action plan in place to prepare for this life event.

So, when should you retire?

How about yesterday, right? The thing is, it's not just about when you *want* to retire, but more importantly it's about when you're *able* to retire. It's important to set an actual target retirement date that feels right. When we set a deadline, we focus on that date, and we work towards that date. It puts pressure on us like a clock counting down, and this pressure creates a sense of urgency to get our financial house in order.

What type of lifestyle do you envision in retirement?

In order to figure out how much money you need to retire, consider what sort of lifestyle you want in retirement. Can you articulate it? Do you plan to live more frugally than you live now, or maintain the same lifestyle? Will you travel, enjoy the arts, go out to dinner with friends, or engage in other activities that will raise your cost of living? No matter how you envision your retirement, you'll need to plan ahead to fund it. Figuring out the life you want to live in retirement can affect how much you spend in retirement, and what sort of cash flow you'll need. Depending on your goals, you might even need to save more than you originally planned.

Retirement planning isn't just about the money - it's also about the things money can't buy. It's important for your financial advisor to learn what's important to you and where you want to be in 5, 10, and 20 years. In order to know how much money you'll need to set aside to retire comfortably, you'll need to clearly define your goals and dreams. Also, many decisions you make can impact your bottom line and the assets available to you in retirement.

Take a moment and think about these questions. Does your vision of retirement include:

- Traveling or vacationing?
- Remodeling your home?
- Spending time with kids and grandkids?
- Taking on a new hobby?
- Moving or relocating?
- Volunteering?
- Working part-time? Going back to school?
- Starting a business?

Most people know planning for retirement is more than just stockpiling a bunch of money and calling it a day. Understanding the fact that your needs may change throughout retirement as you age is an important step in examining whether or not your savings and investments can be sustained, or if you'll need to account for any income gaps.

Do you know which Social Security claiming strategy can maximize your lifetime benefits?

The Social Security Administration provides you with many ways to claim your benefits. The Social Security handbook currently has 2,728 separate rules governing your benefits, yet they don't have a hotline to advise you on the best claiming strategy. Choosing the right benefits at the right time could mean substantial, additional dollars to you in retirement. Making a mistake with your particular claiming strategy could wind up costing you a big slice of your benefits.

It can certainly be advantageous to run an analysis on these numbers to see which option makes sense for you and your family. The Social Security benefit you receive depends on two main factors: what your yearly earnings were while you were working, and when you begin collecting benefits. You can start collecting Social Security benefits from Uncle Sam as early as age 62 (considered early retirement age). Keep in mind that while you can start this cash flow at 62, the sooner you begin, the more checks come, and the lower your monthly benefits amount will be. To get your full benefit, wait until full retirement age (FRA), which is currently 66 but gradually increases to age 67. Here you receive a bigger monthly benefit by delaying but will receive less payments (based on life expectancies). To receive an even bigger monthly payout, you can delay claiming Social Security until age 70.

It's important that you get it right, because soon after you claim, your benefits become permanent - there are no do-overs. The Social Security system is extremely complex, and a better understanding of your claiming options can help optimize your overall retirement dollars. An analysis should be conducted to examine your options and see how they work for your specific situation. This way, you'll know the most efficient strategy to claim your benefits in order to maximize them through retirement.

Do you have a plan in place to address unexpected healthcare expenses that may arise in retirement?

Planning for unexpected expenses in retirement - Medicare expenses, additional healthcare expenses, long-term care expenses - is a must for any retirement plan. Making sure you have emergency money in your plan for a rainy day is also essential. If your needs suddenly change, or you require quick access to capital, having funds set aside for this purpose gives you the flexibility to deal with changing circumstances, and provides you a cushion within your retirement plan.

It's a fact that health care costs have been increasing at a record pace in recent years, and many believe they may continue to rise. Most of us know the old saying, "*there are two certainties in life: death and taxes*," but there's another certainty retirees need to face: rising healthcare costs. Many people don't appreciate the significant impact health care costs can have on their retirement savings. These expenses can cast a shadow over even the best retirement plans.

Many retirees fly blind when it comes to understanding what could potentially be one of their most costly expenses in retirement; they are not financially prepared for the high cost of medical care. Too many people believe that Medicare covers most or all of their medical expenses, without knowing the facts of what is and what isn't covered. Health care expenses are a significant part of retirement spending, and they should be one of your main concerns. By conducting a complete retirement analysis, you can better understand these costs and their effects.

A quick note on Medicare: Medicare isn't free. There's typically no monthly premium for hospital insurance coverage (Part A) if you've paid Medicare taxes while working, but, unless covered by your employer, there is a standard premium for medical insurance (Part B), depending on your income. Further, there's usually a fee that varies for Medicare prescription drug plans. So not only is this an expense you need to plan for, but supplemental Medicare insurance may be a reality you need to address.

Medicare is not designed to cover long-term care expenses, which is a common misconception. As previously mentioned, one of the greatest potential threats to retirement is when a long-term care situation arises. If you won't qualify for Medicaid due to your income and assets, you should seriously look into a long-term care insurance policy for more complete coverage, and try to find room in your budget to pay for it.

What impact can taxes have on your retirement?

Taxes don't disappear when you stop working. In fact, your tax bill can take a big bite out of your retirement income. And for this reason, proper planning is essential.

Taxes on Social Security benefits:

As discussed earlier, most people can begin collecting their Social Security benefits as early as age 62. What's important to remember is that while many states don't tax Social Security benefits, they are counted as taxable income by the federal government. So, depending on your "combined income," (adjusted gross income, plus nontaxable interest earned, plus half of your Social Security benefits), you could end up owing federal income tax on a portion of your Social Security benefits. Currently, up to 85 percent of your Social Security benefits may be taxable if you have income in addition to your benefits. You'd definitely want to consult a tax advisor on this to be sure.

Another note on Social Security in retirement: if you plan on working in retirement, you should also be aware of the impact this additional income has on your Social Security benefits. Social Security has what is called an "earnings test." Essentially it applies only to people below normal retirement age (NRA). If you fall under the NRA, Social Security withholds benefits if your earnings exceed a certain level, called the *retirement earnings test exempt amount.* This number can change and has steadily increased over time. Generally speaking, for example, if your wages exceeded $17,040 in 2018, you'd have a reduction of $1 of Social Security benefits for every $2 you earn over that amount. (Note: there are many types of earnings income that do not count towards the limit.)

As you can see, rules change; so, you want to make sure you're up-to-date with the regulations regarding this matter. For more clarity on this, and its potential impact on your taxable situation, I recommended you speak to a qualified tax advisor.

Taxes on retirement account withdrawals:

After age 59 ½, you can start withdrawing balances from traditional IRAs, 401ks, 403bs, TSPs, etc. without paying the 10% early withdrawal penalty — exceptions are sometimes made in cases of disability, qualified first-time homebuyer distributions, or certain medical expenses. When it comes to taxation of these accounts, keep in mind that you often need to pay federal (and state, if applicable) income tax on these withdrawals — unless it's a Roth IRA held for at least five years, in which contributions have already been taxed. Of course, withdrawal rules can vary depending on plan type, company, institution, and other factors. I recommend seeking professional tax guidance when it comes to understanding the rules affecting your individual situation.

Do you know the appropriate withdrawal strategy to ensure your savings last your lifetime?

If you thought it was hard to grow a nest egg, try living off of one in retirement, where your potential to earn is much less than during your working years. A lot is written about how to build a nest egg, but not as much about taking money out. Many have no idea how potentially risky it can be to withdraw too much from their retirement savings each year. As we transition from career to retirement, more and more people are grappling with this question: how much can I safely withdraw from my nest egg each year without running out of money? Finding an answer to that is like hitting a moving target. The optimal withdrawal rate is dependent upon things like investment performance and inflation.

High withdrawal rates can have a dramatic impact on determining how long an investment portfolio can last in retirement. Several issues should be looked at when figuring out an investor's withdrawal rate. Time horizon and asset allocation objectives are all important factors that can shape how long a portfolio could last. The higher the withdrawal rate, the faster a portfolio can be spent down. The lower the rate, the less likely you are to outlive your investment portfolio during a lengthy retirement.

Next, we need to look at returns on these portfolios. Higher average returns can help extend retirement funds, but you'd be taking on more risk to obtain these returns. Things can get tricky. So, what's an investor to do? A comprehensive retirement analysis should help you see the outcomes with various withdrawal rates, so you can make more educated decisions.

One strategy is to recalculate the amount you may need to pull from your retirement investments each year based upon their year-end value and your life expectancy. This enables you to avoid running out of money too soon by continuing to withdraw a set percentage of assets, even if a market downturn has significantly reduced the value of those assets. Another strategy may be to exchange a portion of your portfolio for an income annuity aimed at providing the needed income, while addressing the longevity situation as well.

Whichever formula you decide to use to tackle this dilemma, financial modeling tools such as those found in financial planning software can prove helpful in calculating withdrawal amounts, and projecting how different rates of return can affect the funds available to you each year.

How can you plan for inflation in retirement?

Do you know if your savings and investments are going to outpace inflation throughout retirement? When it comes to a long retirement, you need to take the necessary steps to make sure your savings last. One way to do this is to structure your investment portfolio to outpace inflation. Inflation risk represents a serious challenge for retirement income planning, and its impact is amplified over an extended period of time. According to the Department of Labor Statistics, the United States inflation rate from 1913 to 2017 has averaged 3.22% per year. If your investments don't grow at a fast-enough pace, your income and nest egg might decrease in value, or may not be able to keep up with these rising costs. Over time, your dollars purchase less goods and services, and savings are consumed faster.

Although you should aim to reduce your exposure to risk in retirement, you still need to invest in a way where your long-term returns get ahead of, or at least keep pace with, inflation. A qualified financial advisor should be able to sit down with you and review your monthly expenses in retirement, include a reasonable rate of inflation in their monthly expense projections, and help position your investment and savings dollars in the correct place to ensure you are keeping up with inflation throughout retirement.

Do you need to use your home equity in retirement? And if so, how?

Many retirees face a shortage between what they saved for retirement and what they actually need to live on. Even with decades of hard work, it can be tough to save up enough cash to cover all your costs in retirement. The largest asset an average couple has entering retirement is likely their home equity, and since many older Americans are property-rich and cash-poor, they could use their home equity to help fund their retirement if or when things get tight. Whether you decide to sell and downsize, take out a reverse mortgage, or tap into your home's equity through a cash-out refinance, a well-thought-out strategy is very important when it comes to using your home to help fund retirement. Should you decide to go down this path, I recommend you start by asking questions, such as:

- Are you having difficulty meeting your monthly expenses?
- Do you want to pay off an existing debt (that has a high interest rate)?
- Do you need to make a home improvement that might increase your quality of life and likely the value of your home?

There is no one-size-fits-all approach, and everyone's situation is different, so it may be wise to consider all options and understand their effects on your retirement plan. Most people don't spend enough time considering how to strategically use their home equity as an income source in retirement. Being creative with your home equity can be beneficial since it may provide much needed cash flow, and even allow you to delay Social Security for a higher monthly benefit.

Do you know how long your money can last in retirement while still maintaining your current standard of living?

Due to increasing life expectancies, many retirees are running into the problem of outlasting their savings. Have you ever wondered how long your money can last in retirement while maintaining your current lifestyle? This is an important question to answer and lies at the heart of retirement income planning. In all my years in the financial services industry, I've found that one of the greatest fears of retirees today is running out of money before they run out of life. Of course, no one can predict with certainty how long they might live. But given today's longer life spans, it's smart to plan as if you're going to live quite a while, maybe longer than you expect. If you base your spending on a shorter life expectancy, and you actually live longer, you could be in for a challenging and stressful retirement.

Knowing this answer becomes more important given the volatility and uncertainty in the financial markets and economy that can significantly impact retirement savings. A simple and general "brush-stroke" formula can be used to try to figure out how long your money can last. However, there are many key factors that need to be examined, such as monthly expenses (inflation adjusted of course), income sources, rates of returns on your retirement savings, withdrawal rates, taxes and Social Security, just to name a few.

A financially comfortable retirement requires lots of planning and preparation. The point of the calculations performed in a comprehensive retirement analysis is to help shed light on this question of how long your money could last, and ultimately to provide a lifetime of income to enjoy a stress-free retirement, knowing you can continue to live life on your terms. Financial planning software allows you to run many different scenarios, so you can better wrap your arms around the probability of your money lasting beyond your lifespan, and not the other way around.

Do you know how big of a nest egg you'll need as you enter retirement? What if your retirement lasts 30 or 40 years?

Thanks to healthier lifestyles and breakthroughs in medical technology, life expectancies for Americans have increased significantly during the past half-century. While it's good news that you can expect to live longer in retirement and have a better quality of life, it also means your investment portfolio may need to last for 30 years or more. Retirement planning is not about planning for average life expectancy; it's about planning for beyond-average life expectancy. While most

Americans now expect to live longer than previous generations, many have not factored longevity into planning for a retirement.

When it comes to retirement planning, conventional wisdom says you'll need to have saved roughly 8 times your pre-retirement annual income, on the low end, in order to maintain your current lifestyle during retirement; and more like 20 times your annual salary on the high-end. I'm not a big believer of conventional wisdom, and believe we can be as good as our options. Obviously, as you have now learned, there are countless aspects, variables and strategies that can affect these projections. Estimating what your retirement expenses can be should provide you with a ballpark figure for the amount of savings you'll need. It won't be perfect because it requires making assumptions about factors such as how long you'll live, what the inflation rate might be, and how your investments could perform. Nevertheless, making an estimate is a valuable exercise - but you still may want to sit with a financial professional to help make sense of it all.

Bottom line, you need to plan. An individualized assessment of your retirement needs is far more valuable than winging it. A detailed retirement analysis can show you the actions to take right now to ensure you don't outlive your assets - no matter how long you live. Financial advisors have the ability to play out various scenarios and look at all of the factors that go into answering the critical question of how big of a nest egg you need to enjoy a long retirement.

Do you know if you're going to have a retirement income shortfall?

In 2017, the National Institute on Retirement Security calculated the nation's retirement shortfall is estimated to be between $6.8 trillion and $14 trillion. Think about that for a moment. This is a staggering amount! As mentioned previously, one of the biggest risks to a comfortable retirement is running out of money too soon. With the repercussions of the Great Recession, market volatility, a Social Security system in need of revamping, and whatever market calamity is looming ahead on the horizon, retirees should plan adequately to overcome the potential shortfalls of retirement income.

Given that life expectancies are on the rise, the risks are only getting greater. Matters are compounded due to the low interest rate environment and expected returns on one's retirement assets, which means it could take more money than ever to retire comfortably. Personally, I feel that a comprehensive retirement analysis performed by a financial advisor is a must. This analysis examines your savings and investments, details your expenses, takes into account your retirement goals, and then determines whether you have a retirement surplus or shortfall.

Do you feel confident your retirement plan is sustainable for you to enjoy a worry-free retirement?

Many people nearing retirement are worried they won't be able to save enough to last them a lifetime. Furthermore, those already in retirement may be worried they'll outlive their nest eggs. The fact is, we're living longer than ever before, and this can dramatically increase financial challenges in retirement – your money needs to last. Increased longevity is a blessing, but an expensive one, because it translates to the need for a bigger retirement nest egg to ensure we get through our twilight years.

In my opinion, the best way to get the right answers to these and many more pressing retirement questions is to work with a financial advisor you trust, that understands your particular situation, goals and needs – and with the use of financial planning and analysis software, can help you better understand how your decisions may affect the options and choices available during your retirement. You may be the greatest statistician, economist, or market prognosticator, but only a comprehensive retirement analysis performed by financial planning software can accurately calculate all of the things mentioned above and help bring it all together.

I use retirement income software with all my clients to analyze their assets, income and expenses. This software produces various detailed scenarios, compares the outcome of each, and presents the optimal retirement strategy. These scenarios consider their goals, taxes, inflation, pension, Social Security, time horizon, risk tolerance and anything else that may be relevant to their specific situation. Ultimately, there is one major question we're always asking: will you have sufficient funds to last in retirement while maintaining the same lifestyle, no matter how long your retirement may be?

If you could know now what the future holds with regards to your retirement, would you want that information today, or would you want it when it's possibly too late to correct or modify your plan? My guess is, you'd want to take control of your financial life and start planning for your retirement today.

CONCLUSION

Taking Control of Your Financial Future

"Spend each day trying to be a little wiser than you were when you woke up." - Charlie Munger

---

Congratulations on joining me through this journey to financial peace of mind. We've covered a lot of ground, and I'm glad you stuck with it from the beginning to the end. I sincerely appreciate the time you've taken to go down this road in learning the *Plan Smart, Retire Right* approach.

Plan Smart, Retire Right isn't just the title of this book. It represents a framework for what smart retirement planning is all about. It represents the steps you can take, and the relief you can gain, by creating your own stress-free retirement. I know we've discussed a lot of information in this book, and it's a lot to process in such a short period of time. As you can see, however, there's a lot more to learn! Much of what I've covered has significant depth to it, and it's almost impossible to cover everything in detail. That's why I strongly suggest meeting with an advisor to help set you down the best path to your own stress-free retirement.

There are plenty of people out there that can speak intelligently on how to grow and invest your money over the long-term. Many of them have great ideas, and even do great things. While obtaining good returns on your money is important, as you get older, the steps you take to protect this money are what matters most. My advice is for you to find someone who can help with the growth aspects of your retirement funds, as well as the risk management side.

I wrote this book because I wanted to share the processes and strategies that have benefitted my clients, which are the same strategies that have helped thousands achieve their own stress-free retirement. Over the years, I've seen many people make critical mistakes with their money which could've been easily avoided. Critical mistakes in planning can derail the retirement you've always envisioned. I am confident that *Plan Smart, Retire Right* can help facilitate a stress-free retirement for you, filled with financial success and peace of mind.

I suppose I didn't have to write this book, and I could've just continued sharing this stress-free retirement system with my clients, but I have a bigger purpose. I've decided to combine my passion for what I do with my years of broad-based financial knowledge to create this book and to share it with the world, in order to help people create the retirement lifestyle they deserve. If you follow the concepts I've outlined in this book, I believe you, too, can experience the inner peace that comes from knowing you've protected your nest egg from the unknowns in life, and created an abundance of income, so you'll never have to worry about running out of money in retirement.

While there is no doubt you've gained tremendous value from reading this book, the true value comes from taking an active role towards realizing a more stress-free retirement. The key is for you to take action today. Whatever you do, don't wait. Don't put it off until tomorrow. The time will never be just right. Take the first step. Make a commitment to yourself to reevaluate your current financial situation, put a plan in place, and set yourself up for true financial freedom.

I thank you from the bottom of my heart for taking time out of your busy schedule to read this book. I hope these strategies and principles make a true difference in your life, and in retirement.

I'd love to hear your thoughts and success stories. Please feel free to drop me a note to tell me how you're doing, and how *Plan Smart, Retire Right* may have changed your life. You can reach me at rich@braviasfinancial.com.

Cheers to *your* stress-free retirement!

ABOUT THE AUTHOR

Richard Zeitz, the founder and President of Bravias Financial, is a graduate of Pennsylvania State University and a veteran in the financial services arena since 1994. As a proud member of the National Ethics Association, his firm is built on the foundation of trust, integrity, and best practices. He has become a thought leader in the industry having written guides and articles focused on retirement planning strategies, which have been featured or quoted in various publications and has been seen on: *US News and World Report, Investopedia, Yahoo! Finance, The Street, MarketWatch, ABC, CBS, FOX, NBC,* and *The National Financial Educators Council.*

In addition to conducting educational workshops and seminars, he frequently speaks to various organizations about wealth management and retirement readiness. Richard also invests time mentoring and educating other financial advisors across the country, sharing his philosophy and approach.

When not helping clients plan for a stress-free retirement, he enjoys theater, traveling with his family, golfing, fishing, and watching his beloved Philadelphia sports teams attempt to put together a championship season.

DISCLOSURES AND DISCLAIMERS

Bravias Financial is an independent retirement planning firm. Investment Advisory Services offered through Bravias Capital Group, LLC, a New Jersey State Registered Investment Adviser. Bravias Capital Group, LLC and Bravias Financial, LLC are independent entities.

The views and opinions expressed herein are those of Richard Zeitz only. Prior and subsequent opinions may differ. The views are provided for the general information of the reader. They are not intended to be specific advice or recommendations to any one individual and should not be interpreted as such. The book and the material contained herein should not be construed as an offer to sell or the solicitation of an offer to buy any security or insurance product or strategy.

This book does not constitute a personal recommendation or take into account the particular investment objectives, financial situation, or needs of potential clients. Advice, if any, given in the book is not intended to be advice concerning tax matters and cannot be relied upon. A decision to execute any financial strategy, investment or purchase of any financial product should be made carefully after a thorough review of the recommendation which includes consultation with your financial, legal and tax professionals. Richard Zeitz has taken reasonable measures to ensure the accuracy of the information contained herein. However, the information and graphics published may contain technical inaccuracies or typographical errors and therefore is provided "as is" without any warranty of any kind.

When addressing financial matters in this book, we've taken every effort to ensure the accuracy represented with regards to products and services, and their ability to improve your finances to grow your money over time. However, there is no guarantee that you will see any results or earn any money using any of their ideas, tools, strategies or recommendations, and we don't promote any get-rich-quick schemes in any of our content. Nothing in this book is a promise or guarantee of earnings or results. Your level of success in attaining similar results is dependent upon a number of factors including your skill, knowledge, ability, dedication, savvy, and financial situation, to name a few. Because these factors differ according to individuals, we cannot and don't guarantee your success, income level, or ability to grow your money. You alone are responsible for your actions and results in retirement. Any forward-looking statements, projections or examples outlined in this book or any of our sites are simply our opinion and thus are not guarantees or promises for actual performance or results.

Investments involve risk including the potential loss of principal, and unless otherwise stated, are not guaranteed. No investment strategy, such as asset allocation or diversification can guarantee a profit or protect against loss in periods of declining values. Please note that rebalancing investments may cause investors to incur transaction costs and, when rebalancing a non-retirement account, taxable events could be created that may increase your tax liability. Rebalancing a portfolio cannot show a profit or protect against a loss in any given market environment.

Variable insurance and annuity product are considered securities products and require one to have proper FINRA registrations, in addition to proper state insurance licensing, prior to selling or discussing such products. Fixed annuities are long-term investment vehicles. Early withdrawals may result in tax liabilities, penalties and could be subject to surrender charges. These charges may result in a loss of bonus, indexed interest and fixed interest, and a partial loss of your principal. Bonus annuities may include an annuitization requirement, lower capped returns, or other restrictions that are not included in similar annuities that don't offer a premium bonus feature. Riders are available at an additional cost and are subject to conditions, restrictions and limitations, and benefits are generally not available as a lump sum payout. Insurance products and services are offered through individually licensed and appointed agents in various jurisdictions. Any mention of guarantees are backed by the financial strength and claims-paying ability of the issuing insurance company. NOT FDIC INSURED. NOT BANK GUARANTEED. MAY LOSE VALUE, INCLUDING LOSS OF PRINCIPAL. NOT INSURED BY ANY STATE OR FEDERAL AGENCY.

Made in the USA
Middletown, DE
22 February 2019